CRICUT ACCESSORIES

THE COMPLETE GUIDE TO MASTERING YOUR CRICUT MACHINE AND IMPROVE IT WITH ACCESSORIES AND TOOLS.

Made with love

by

Sienna

Tally

Table of Contents

Introduction

First of all, thank you for purchasing this "Cricut Accessories" guide. As you can understand from the name, this book is not dedicated to understanding and using a specific Cricut model (for more information about this, you can visit my bibliography, where you can find other guides explicitly created for each model of Cricut released until today!) In this guide, it doesn't matter if you are an expert in crafting or just starting. We will start enriching your skills and your cultural background together.

If you are reading this book, it means you know what Cricut is and what it is used for. Perhaps it's the "how" that brought you here. However, for posterity's sake, Cricut is the brand name for an array of scrapbooking home cutters.

It is also the name used to categorize Provo Craft & Novelty Inc. projects, otherwise known as Provo Craft. Anyone who has these gizmos in their apartments uses them for various things, but particularly for cutting paper, felt, vinyl, fabrics, and other materials, including fondant.

Often, paper artisans have Cricut in their workshops alongside many other electronic cutting tools. You will also find this device with card makers and scrapbookers.

The machine has different models, inclusive of which is the Cricut Maker. This particular model is used in friendship with the Cricut

Design Space, cloud-based online software that will be the main focus of this book.

The software is not a lone wolf but needs an internet connection and a device - either a Personal Computer or smartphone. Be as that may, there is an offline version of Cricut Design Space you can use with your phone. Whether it's an Android device, iPad, or iPhone, the space is available for you to use.

The Cricut Maker itself is a versatile machine with interchangeable cutting and marking heads, literally a goldmine of an asset to many material cutting entrepreneurs out there. It has different versions you can use, depending on the kind of project you are working on and the set of features that best help you achieve your design goals.

Chapter 1
Setting Up Your Cricut Machine

Setting up your Cricut machine is more like unwrapping a Christmas present! You have to be careful, but at the same time, you're eager to get started with it. The machine setup of any Cricut machine won't take you more than an hour, and there are a few tools that come with the Cricut machine to guide your installation.

Here, we will be using the Cricut Maker to explain the machine setup seeing as it is the newest Cricut technology available.

Tools Needed

- Cricut Maker.
- Power cord and USB cable.
- Fine point pen.

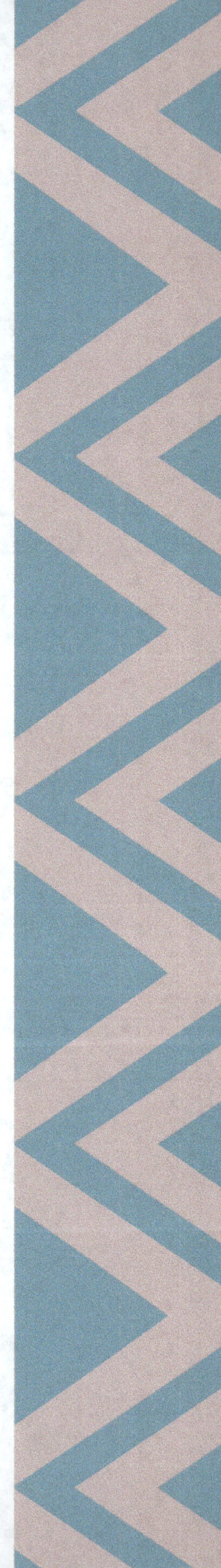

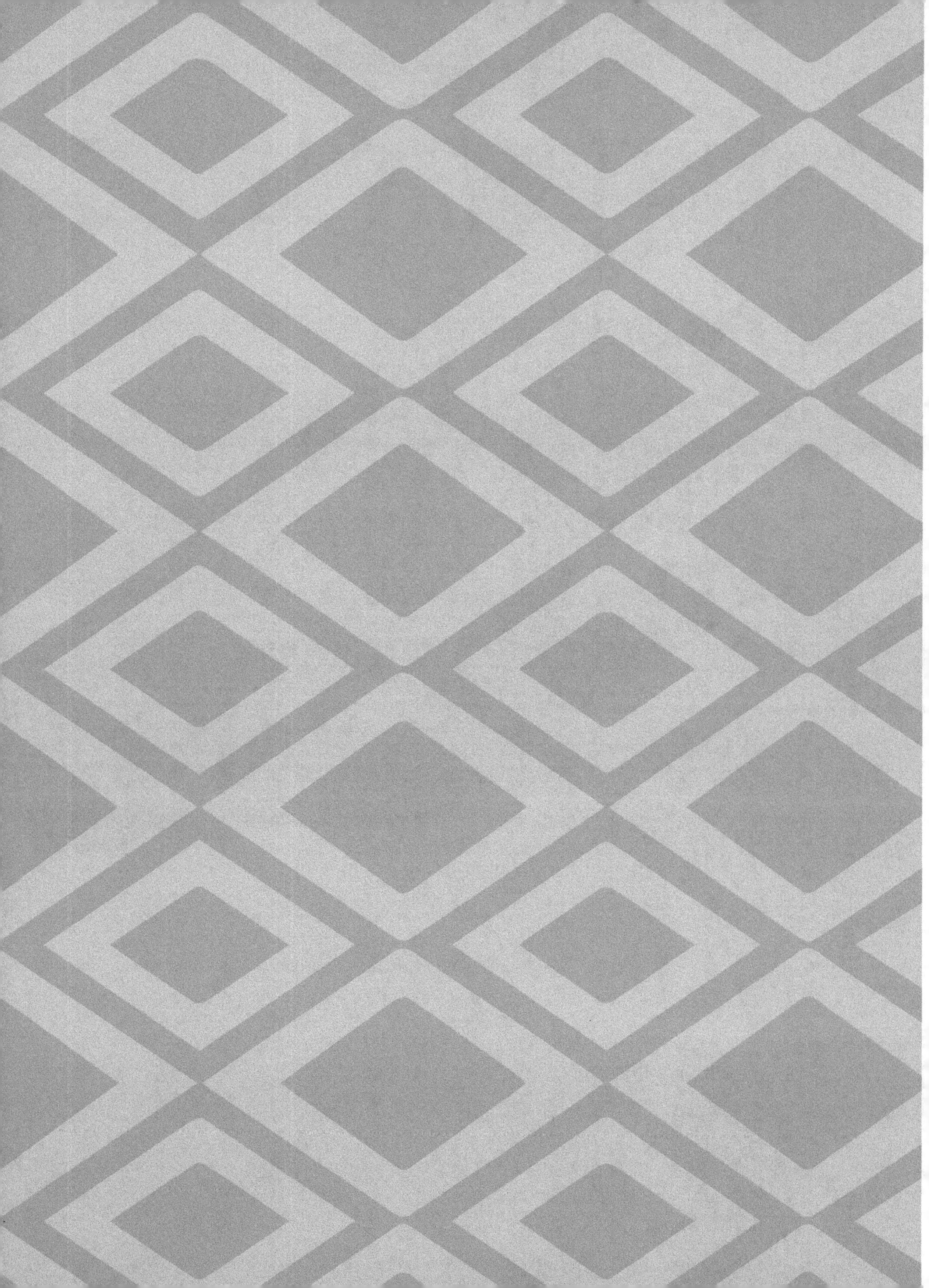

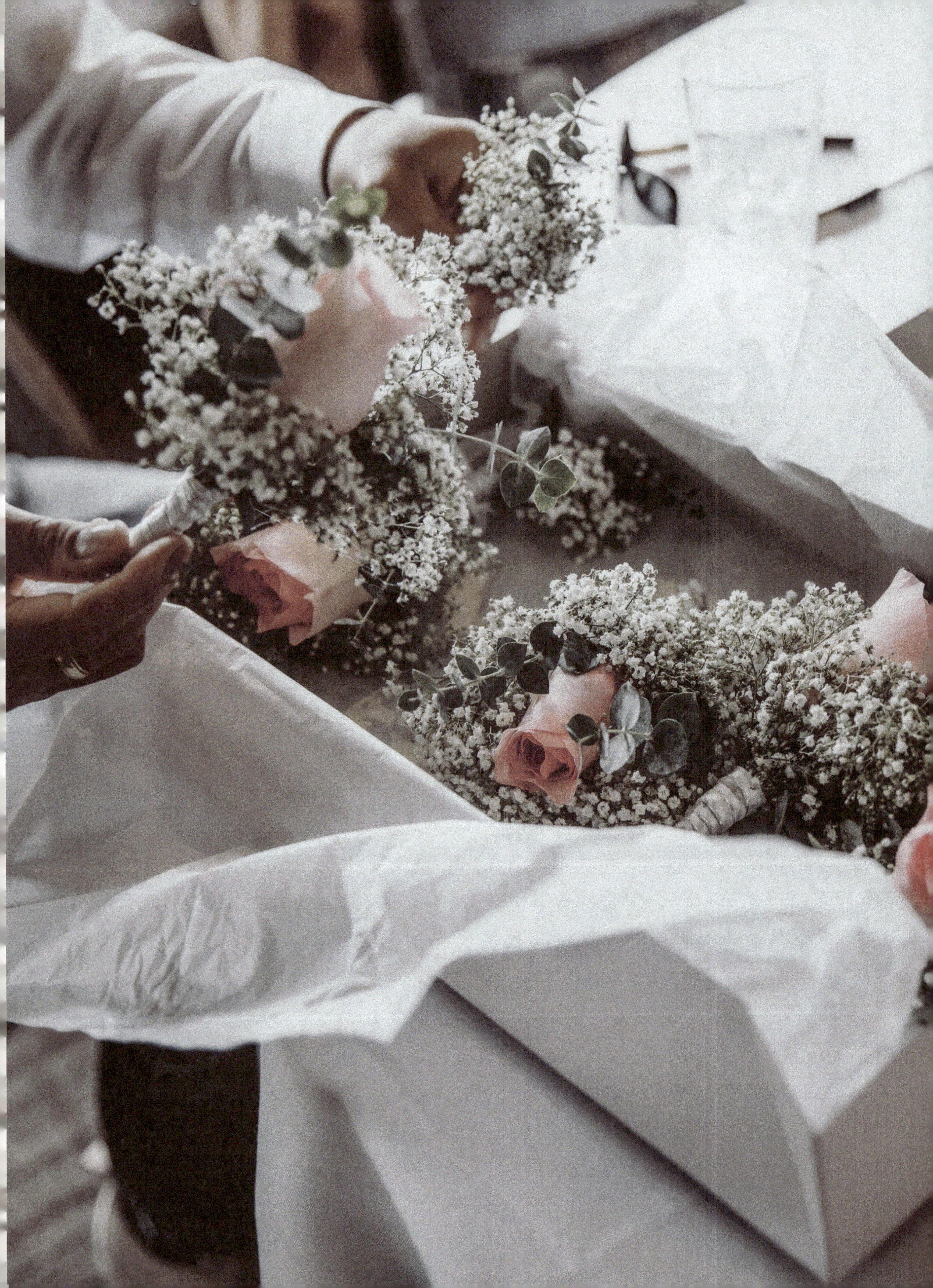

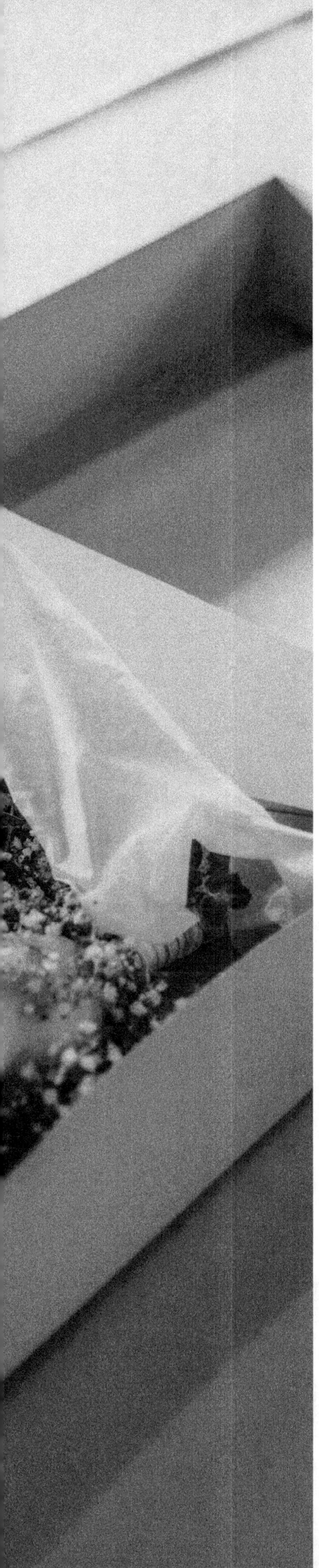

- A fair point blade.
- Rotatory blade with housing.
- LightGrip Mat 12″ by 12″.
- FabricGrip Mat 12″ by 12″.
- A computer, tablet, or mobile phone connected to the internet.

Opening the Box

When you purchase a bundle from Cricut, you will receive a few boxes, but the most significant box amongst them will hold the Cricut Maker. To recognize it, you'll see the picture of the Maker on the box.

When opening the Cricut box, the first thing you see is the welcome packet placed on the machine. The welcome package contains a welcome book, a rotary blade with cover, a fine point pen, a USB cable, and a packet with your first project.

When you take the Cricut machine out of the box, the power cord will be underneath along with the cutting mats.

Unwrapping

The Cricut machine is wrapped with a layer of cellophane and a protective wrapper. Before setting up the device, you have to remove the wrappings.
Some Styrofoam protects the in-housing of the machine, and that has to go too.
Your Cricut Maker will also come with some supplies, and you should unwrap them and check them out. Lucky for you, the fine point blade is already installed in the Cricut Maker, so you don't have to bother with that.

Visit cricut.com/setup

The next step in setting up your machine lies in the technical aspects. Cricut has a webpage dedicated to walking you through this process, which makes it super easy.

Open cricut.com/setup on your device. You can use any device that is compatible with Cricut, like a smartphone, tablet, or computer. When you do that, you will be asked to install Cricut Design Space and also sign up. Then,

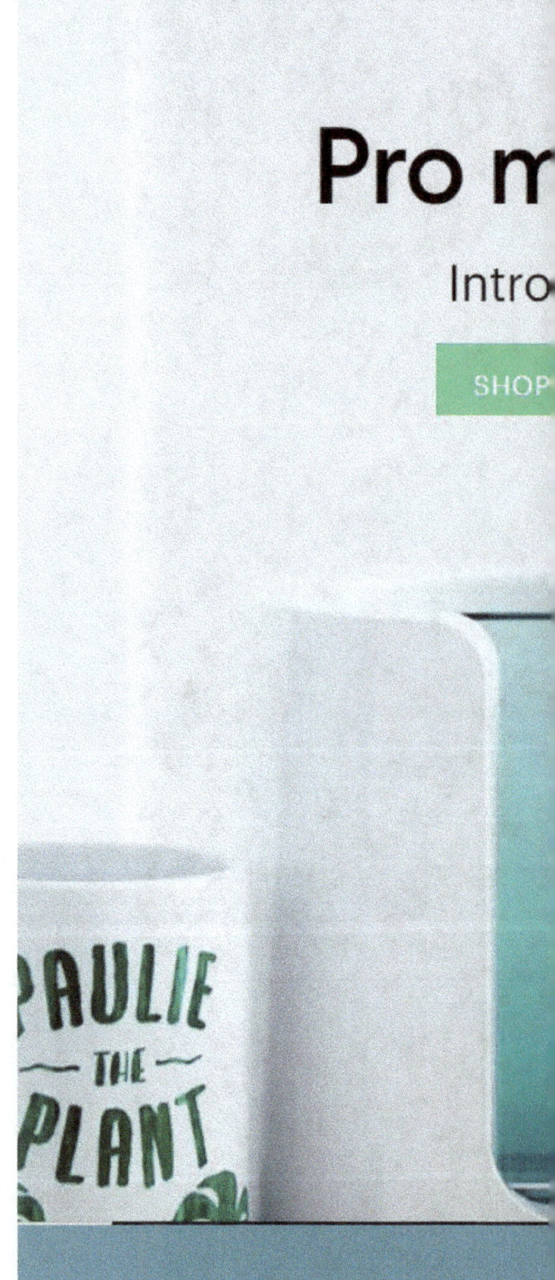

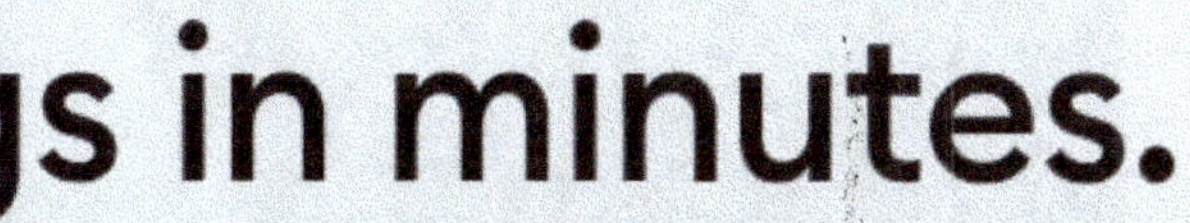

Products   Projects

Shop   Design

gs in minutes.

g Cricut Mug Press™.

MUG PRESS   LEARN MORE

cricut

you'll be given your Cricut ID.
If you have been using a former Cricut machine before, you can carry on with your previous ID.

Plugging It In

Next, you need to take your USB cord and the power cord to power up your Cricut machine.
This will be shown on the setup wizard of the webpage.

For the USB cord, you connect the square end to the Cricut Maker device and the other end to the computer. And, the power cord is easy to connect the Cricut Maker to the power outlet.

Claim Your Bonus

After plugging in your Cricut, you will be able to claim a free welcome bonus from Cricut, which is a free month of Cricut Access. This means that you get to enjoy access to projects, fonts, and Cricut Cut Files.

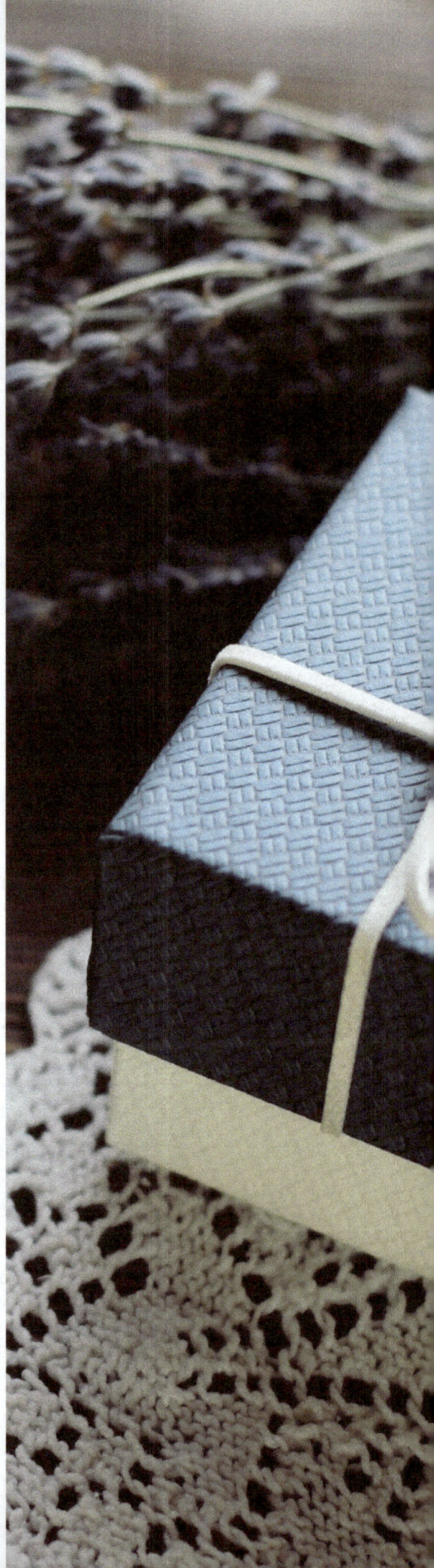

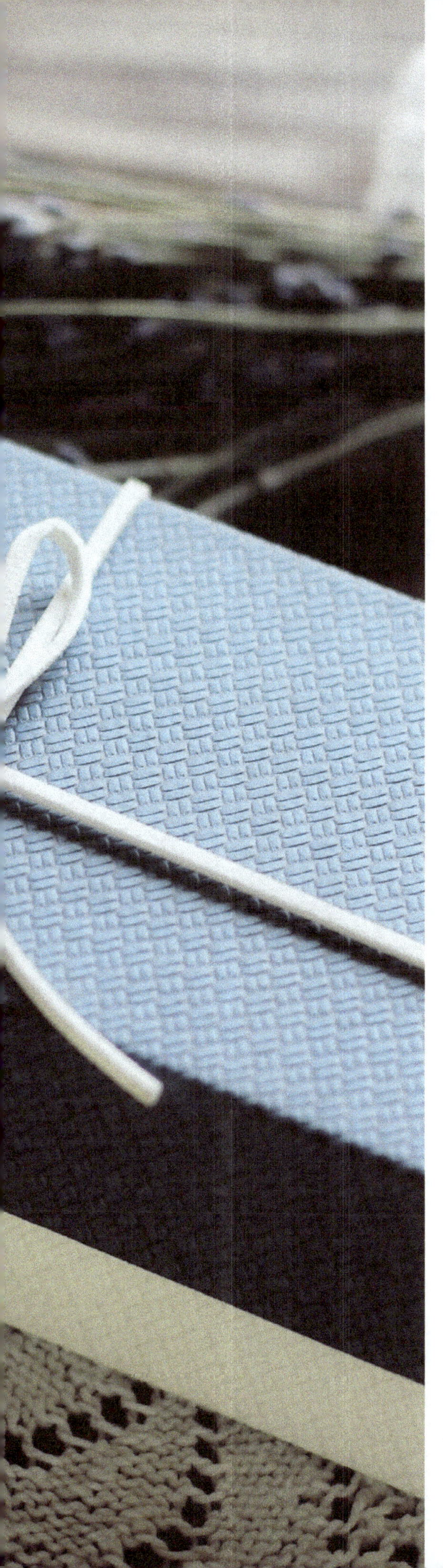

Begin Your Project

If you need a little something to practice before starting your intended project, Cricut Maker machines usually come with a bit of project in the welcome pack to help you get acquainted with the tools.

The Maker comes with all the tools you need to complete the project, which is usually the task of making a little card.

After this, then you can begin using it. The thing is, when you want to use your Cricut Maker, you need to learn how to use Cricut Design Space.

Chapter 2
Cricut accessories and tools for Cricut machines

Cricut cutting machines come with quite a few accessories that you can purchase to add to your machine's functionality. There are some accessories that most of the devices can use and others that are designed only for a specific machine.

The following accessories list will explain what the items are used for and what machines they can be used on.

Cricut BrightPad

The Cricut BrightPad is a convenient device for severe crafters, as it illuminates projects to help with weeding, tracing, quilt blocks, paper piecing, and more. It can even help with jewelry making or model building.

The price is approx-$ 100.

The BrightPad is compatible with all of the Cricut machines and crafting materials.

Cricut BrightPad Is Compatible With:

All makes and models of Cricut Cutters.

Cricut BrightPad Is Not Compatible With:

There are no Cricut machines that the device cannot be used alongside.

Cricut Cartridges

Cricut Cartridges are small cartridges that fit into the slots of some of the older Cricut machines (the Explore Air 2 still has a slot for them). These cartridges were filled with images for purchase to expand a crafting image library.

You no longer need cartridges with current machines, and that is why Cricut has discontinued them. You can purchase digital cartridges from the Cricut craft shop website.

Like the physical cartridges, digital cartridges are sold in batches, which means you have to buy what comes with the pack. However, Design Space has thousands of images, projects, and more that you can buy as individual items when creating your projects.

For those who already have cartridges, they are still able to be used. Design Space still supports them by letting you link cartridges once they have been loaded into the machine.

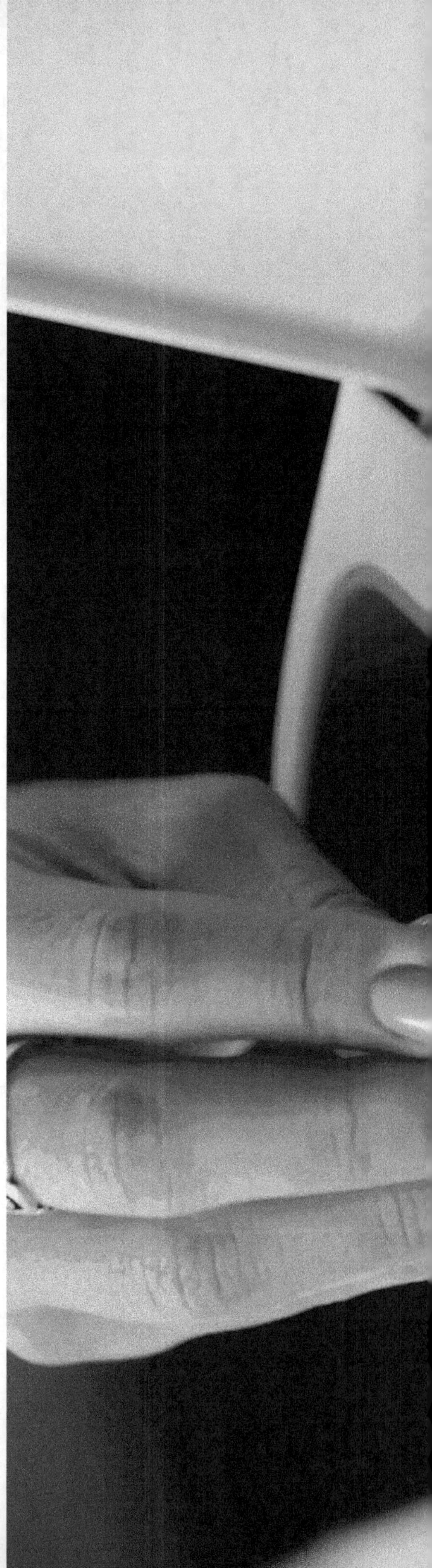

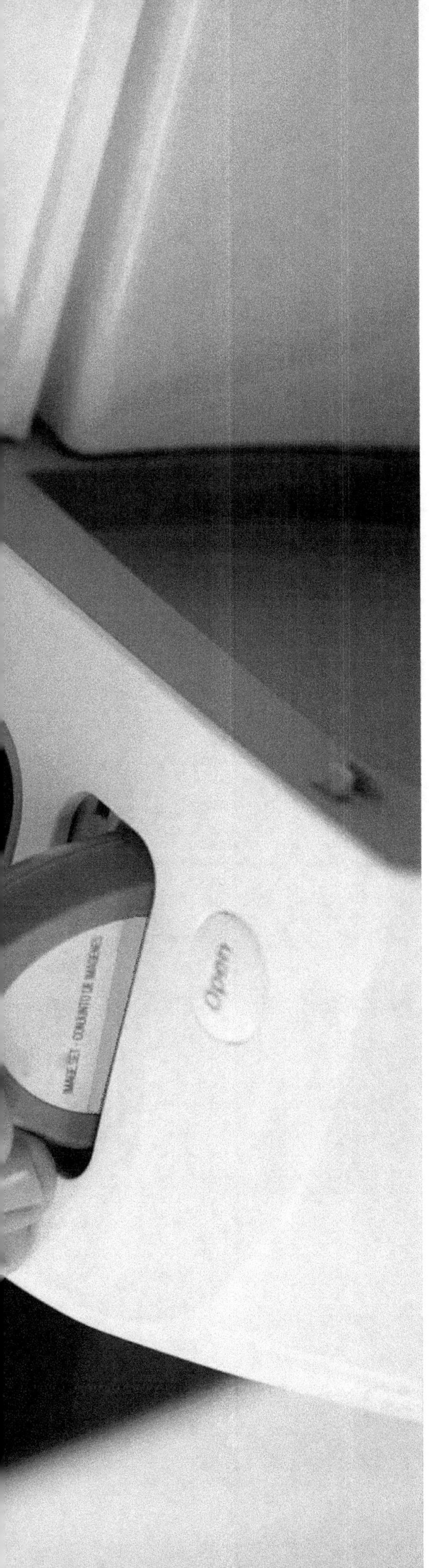

Although the Cricut Maker does not have a slot for cartridges, you can buy the Cricut USB cartridge adaptor for use with your purchased cartridges.

The Cricut Joy does not use cartridges, and you cannot use the Cricut USB cartridge adapter with it.

Cricut Cartridges Are Compatible With:

- Cricut Explore
- Cricut Explore Air
- Cricut Explore Air 2
- Most older and legacy Cricut cutting machine models

Cricut Cartridges Are Not Compatible With:

- Cricut Joy
- Cricut Maker (it needs an adaptor)
- Cricut Cuttlebug

Cricut Craft Tools

The Cricut craft tools have been specifically designed to make crafters' tasks a lot easier. As they are designed around the Cricut cutting machines, they make tasks like extra cutting, weeding, tweezing, tracing, etc., a breeze.

Each of these tools, cutters, rulers, pens, knife blades, and so on can be purchased individually or in various toolsets/bundles.

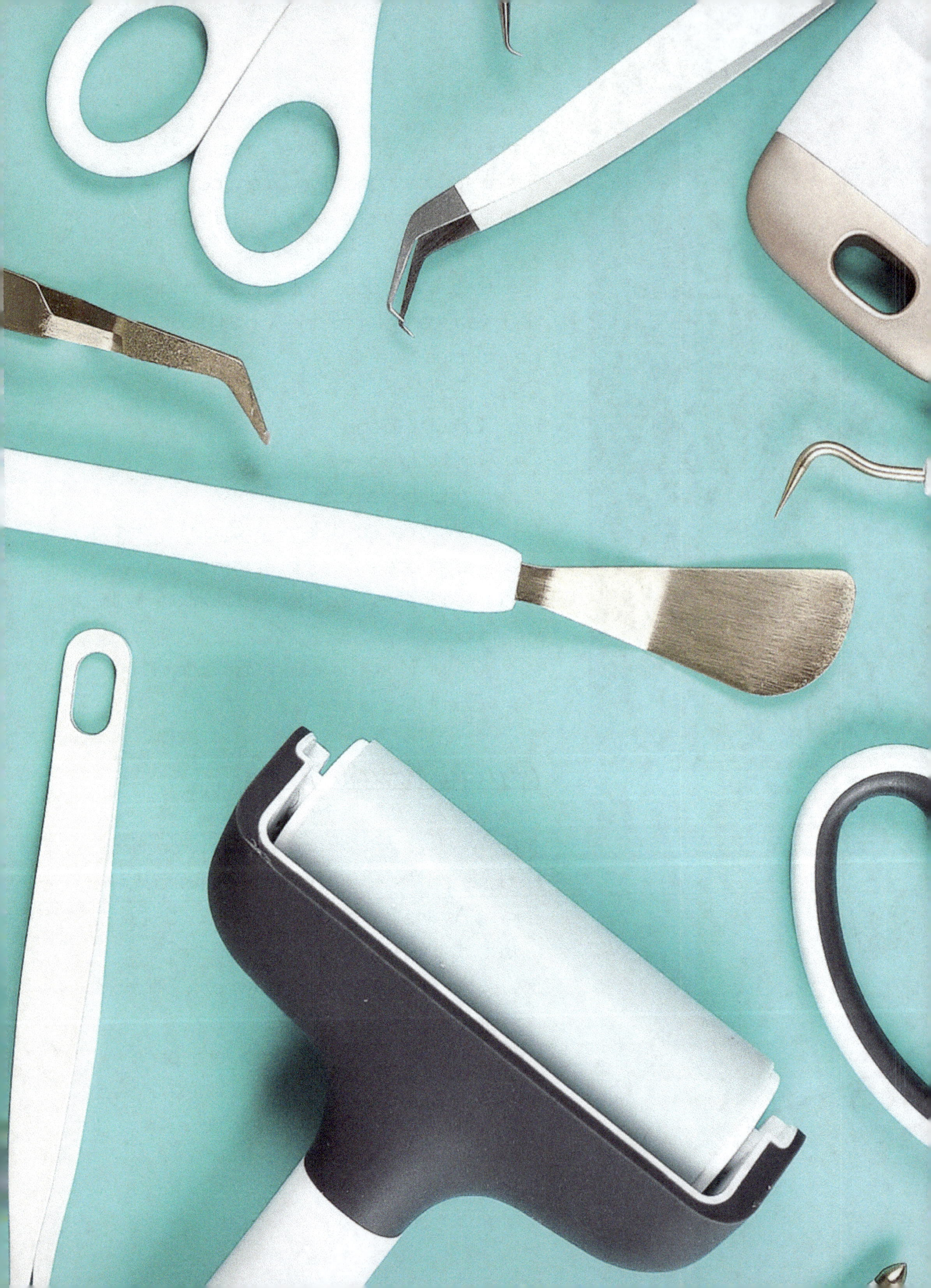

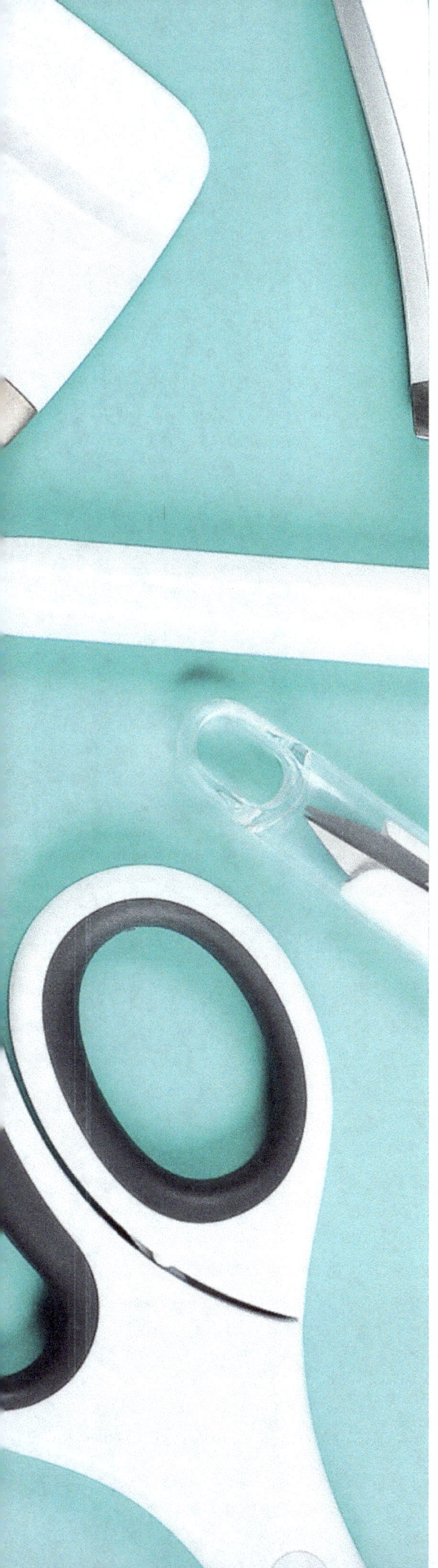

Most Cricut tools come in standard colors such as cream or grey. There are exceptions and special promotions that may change the colors of the tools.

Cricut Tools Are Compatible With:

All makes and models of Cricut Cutters.

Cricut Tools Are Not Compatible With:

There are no Cricut machines that the tools cannot be used alongside. The only tool that is not compatible with every cutting machine is the Cricut Stylus pen.

Cricut Tool Colors

Cricut tools do come in different colors, which include:

- Blue
- Mint
- Gray
- Lilac
- Rose
- Pink
- Peach

Not all of the tools come in these colors, and the coloring can differ depending on the tool type.

Cricut Brayer

The brayer tool looks a bit like a lint roller. Although it does not remove lint, fluff, etc., it helps stick the material firmly and smoothly to cutting mats.
The brayer helps the user to smooth the material and press it firmly down onto cutting mats. It quickly gets rid of wrinkles, kinks, bubbles and can link blocks.
The price is approx-$ 20.

Cricut Distresser

This tool looks like the Cricut Scraper tool, except that it has two slits on either side of it. The distresser is used to give the paper a textured edge.
- Cricut Fabric Shears
- Cricut fabric shears cut through most fabric with ease, and this includes layered materials. The fabric shears are extra sharp with precision blades made from stainless steel.
- They come with both right, and left-handed comfort grip handles.

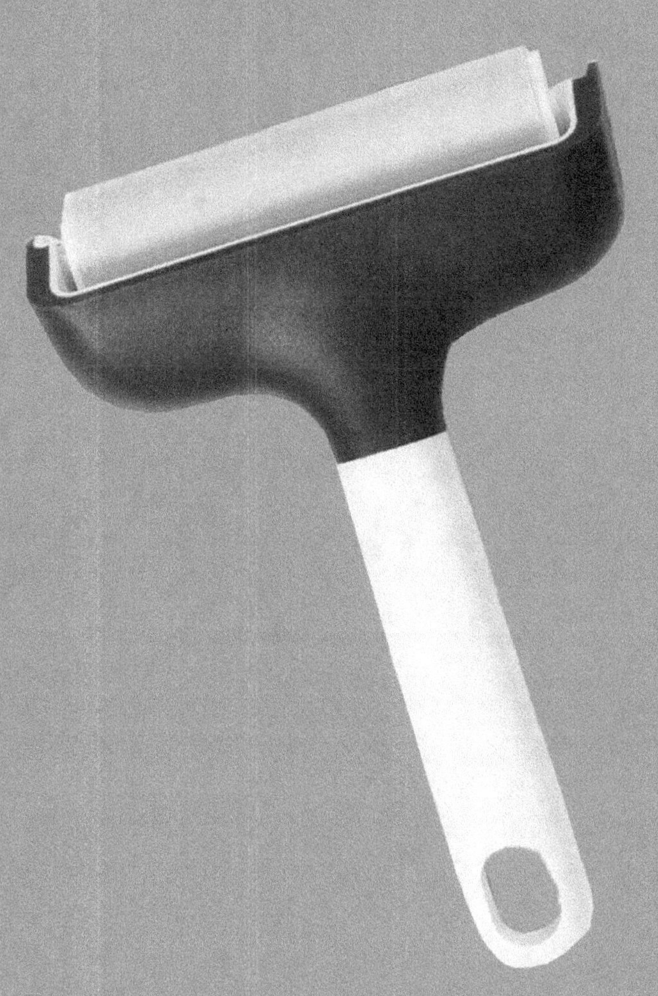

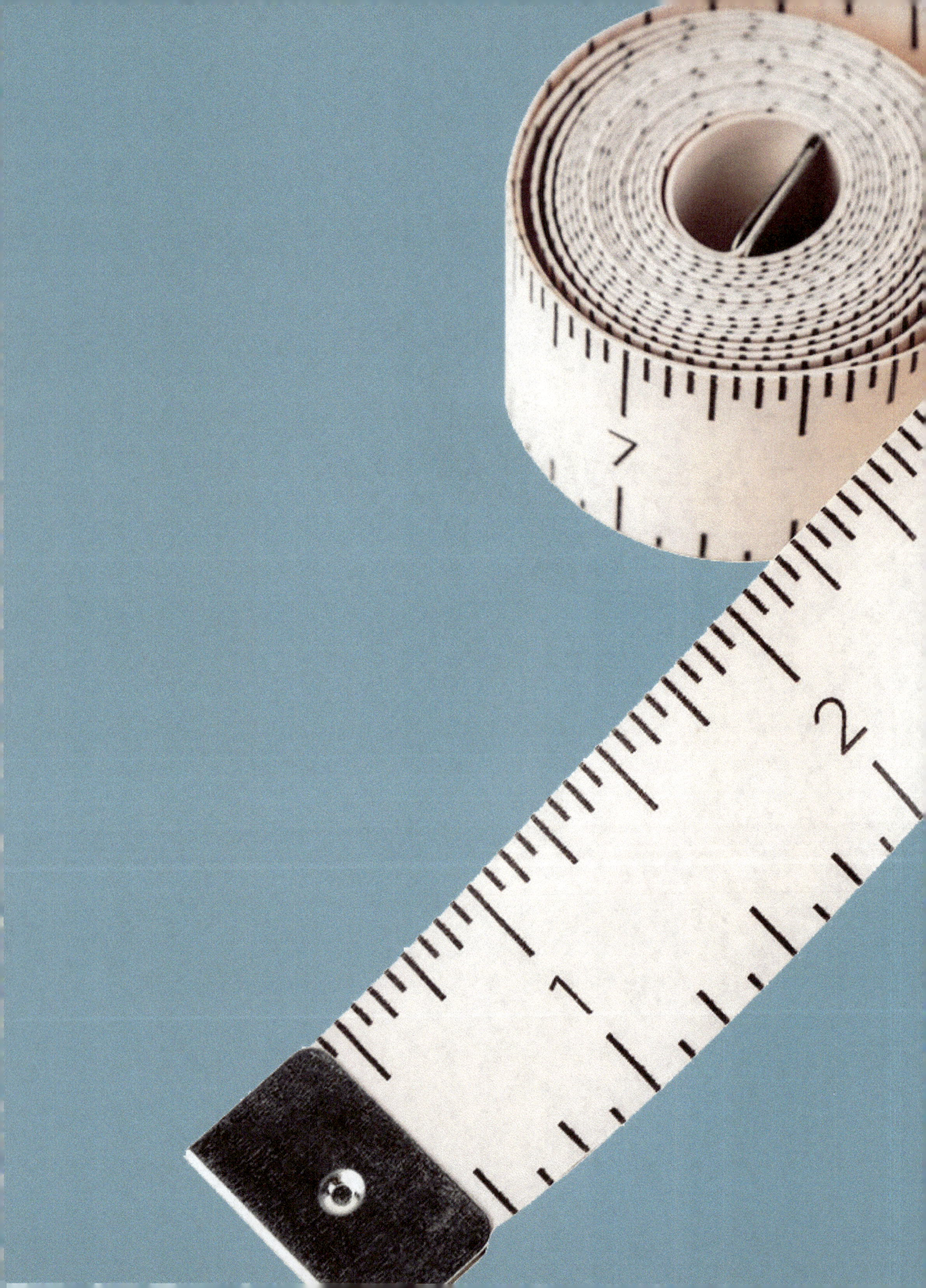

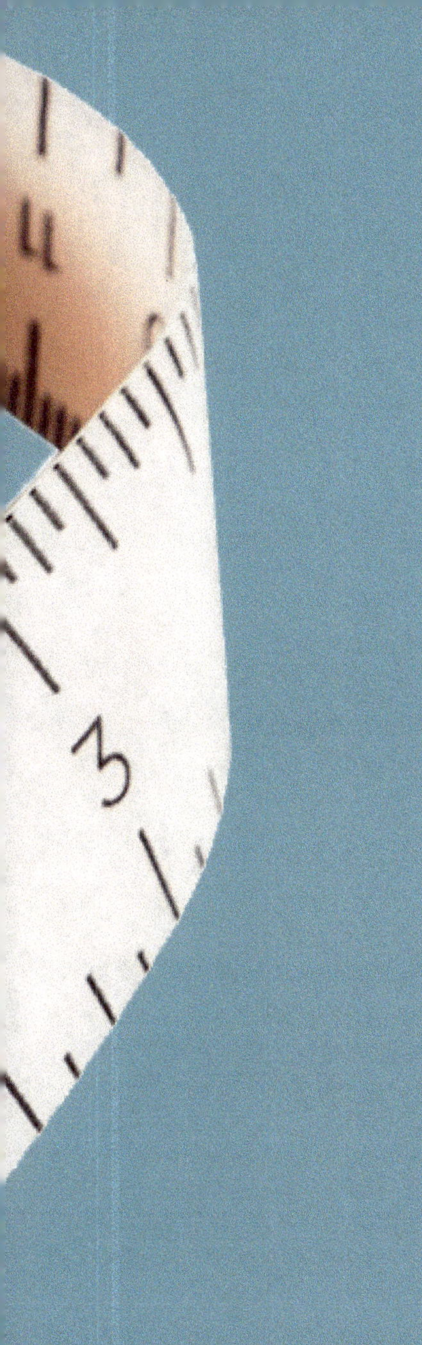

- Cricut Leather Thimble
- Cricut has cute leather thimbles to protect fingers when sewing.
- Cricut Pin Cushion and Pins
- Cricut Pincushion is soft and durable with a set of matching pins to help with sewing crafts.
- Cricut Precision Piercer

This tool usually comes standard as part of the paper crafting toolset. You will need it if you are working with paper crafting for making flowers, swans, etc. The Precision piercer allows crafters to put cuts, tiny holes, and other embellishments in the paper.

Cricut Quilting Tool

The quilting tool is one that most scrapbookers find incredibly useful. This tool creates professional look spirals and twirls that add extra polish to a project.

Cricut Measuring Tape

The Cricut measuring tape measures up to 60". It is a standard fabric measuring tape with the same measurements that you will find on the Design Space screen. This makes it easier to get the designs right for professional-looking craft finishes.

Cricut Rotary Cutter

The Cricut rotary cutter comes in two different sizes, which are 45 mm and 60 mm. They have a carbon alloy steel rotary blade that slices through fabric like a knife through butter.

This is an excellent tool for precision slices of vinyl, leather, and most fabrics. The blade is replaceable. As the head can slide from left to right, it suits both left-handed and right-handed crafters.

Cricut Rulers

Cricut has a few different sized cutting rulers to make crafting more precise and professional to make crafters' lives easier.

The cutting rulers sizes include:
18" x 24" ruler with a stainless steel straight cutting edge, non-slip base, and a protective grip.
12" x 24" clear acrylic design ruler
6" x 26" clear acrylic design ruler
3" x 18" clear acrylic design ruler

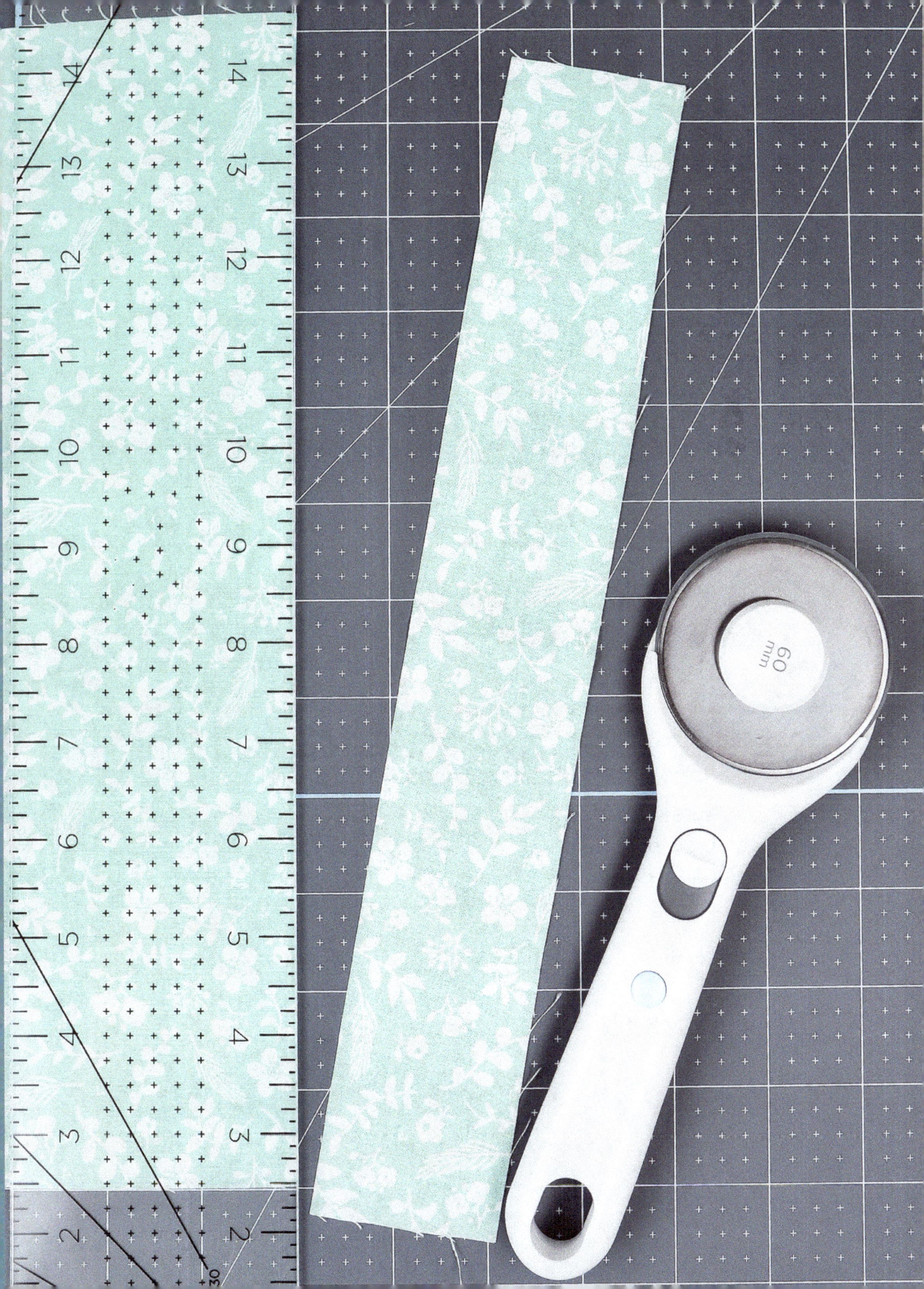

Cricut Scissors

The Cricut scissors are sharp 5" scissors that are ideal for any material, and they come with a protective case to protect the blades. They easily cut through the vinyl, faux leather, paper, cardstock, and more.
They come with a left-handed or right-handed comfort grip handle.

Cricut Scoring Stylus Pen

The Scoring Stylus pen is used for making fold lines in gift boxes, envelopes, and gift cards.
The Cricut Scoring Stylus pen can be used by hand to create folds. It can also be used in the following Cricut cutting machines to create folds with a cut:
- Cricut Explore
- Cricut Explore Air
- Cricut Explore Air 2
- Cricut Maker

Cricut Scraper

The Cricut Scraper comes in a few diffe-

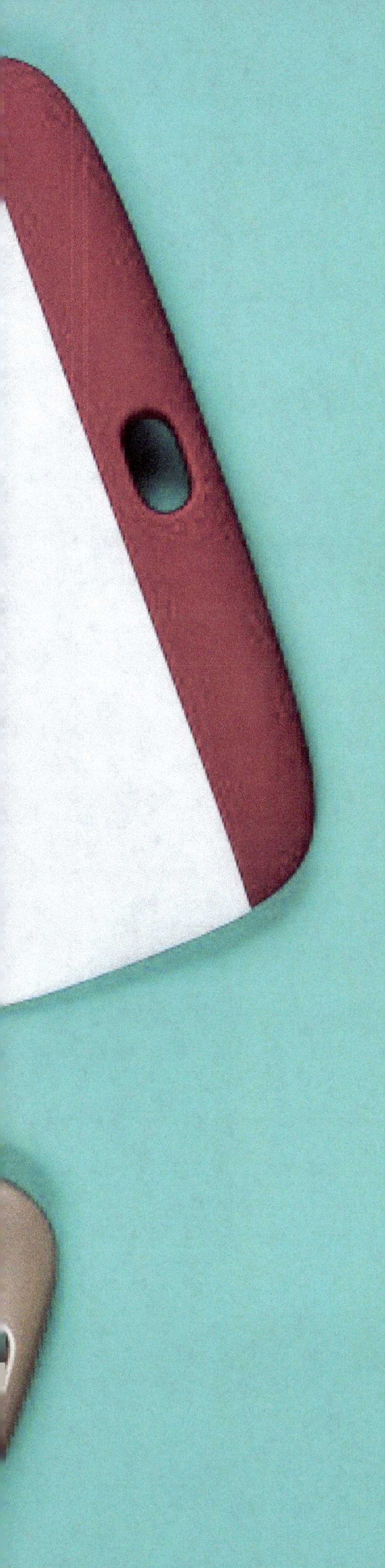

rent sizes; small, medium, and large. It is designed to help prolong the Cricut cutting mats' life as it scrapes unwanted material off the surface.

This is also an excellent tool to use if you do not have a brayer tool, as it is a useful burnishing tool. Suppose you need to make sure that vinyl sticks down securely and runs the scraper over it before pulling off the transfer sheet.

Cricut Seam Ripper

This little tool allows for easy and effective removal of tiny stitches and seams without causing damage to the fabric.

Cricut Spatula

This little tool is a savior when you want to pick up an intricate cut. The tool allows a person to gently get under the image and lift it without tearing it. It is also a handy tool for getting off pieces that have become stuck on the mat or baking sheet.

Cricut Thread Snips

The Cricut Thread Snips are sharp little snipping tools that quickly snip thread or end pieces to neaten them up.

Cricut Trimmer

The Cricut Trimmer is a portable 12" trimmer with a precision blade and a 15" swing-out arm. The swing-out arm makes it easy to measure any type of material while the blade cuts effortlessly with precision through the material(s).
There are blade replacements available in case the trimmer becomes blunt.

Cricut TrueControl Knife

The TrueControl Knife works pretty much the same as a carpenter's knife does. It has a lock-in adjustable blade for more material cutting control and interchangeable blade sizes.
This knife can cut through a host of different materials, including:
*   Vinyl
*   Cardstock
*   Canvas
*   Fabrics

- Leather
- Paper

Cricut Tweezer

There are a few kinds of tweezers offered by Cricut, and these include:
Cricut Broadtip Tweezers - The Cricut Broadtip tweezers are ideal for material crafting and lifting stubborn material from the cutting board. They are also useful for lifting delicate cuts that the spatula may not be able to lift.
Cricut Fine tip Tweezers - These tweezers have an excellent edge that is needed for small intricate cuts that need to be cleaned up or stuck down.
Cricut Hook Tweezers - The hook tweezers can get into those awkward bends and twirls of some craft cuts. They are also suitable for removing larger craft pieces.

Cricut Weeder

The weeder looks like a little hook and is ideal for weeding out (neating) cut image designs. There are two different styles of weeders: the classic weeder and hook weeder. Although the classic weeder is an excellent starter weeder and one that all crafters need, more serious crafters will find the hook

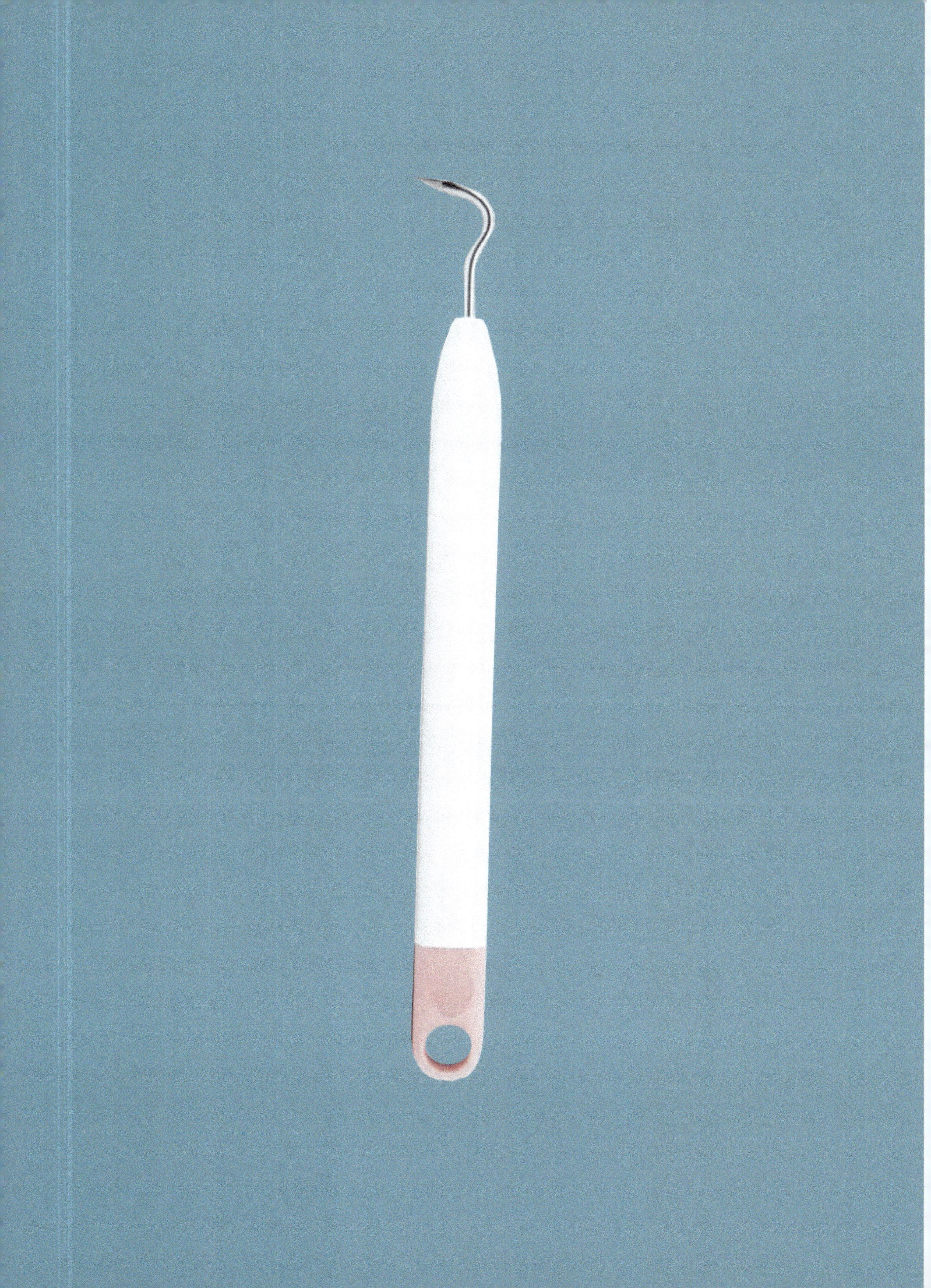

weeder useful for those intricate designs.

Cricut Basic Tool Kit

The Cricut Basic tool kit includes the following tools:

- Cricut scissors
- Cricut Fine tip tweezers
- Cricut classic weeding tool
- Cricut scraper (small)
- Cricut spatula

Cricut Fabric/Sewing Tool Kit

The Cricut Fabric/Sewing tool kit includes the following tools:

- Cricut fabric shears
- Cricut seam ripper
- Cricut leather thimble
- Cricut measuring tape
- Cricut snipper
- Cricut pincushion
- Cricut pins
- Cricut brayer tool
- Cricut Broadtip tweezers

Cricut Starter Tool Kit

The Cricut Starter tool kit includes the following tools:

- Cricut classic weeding tool

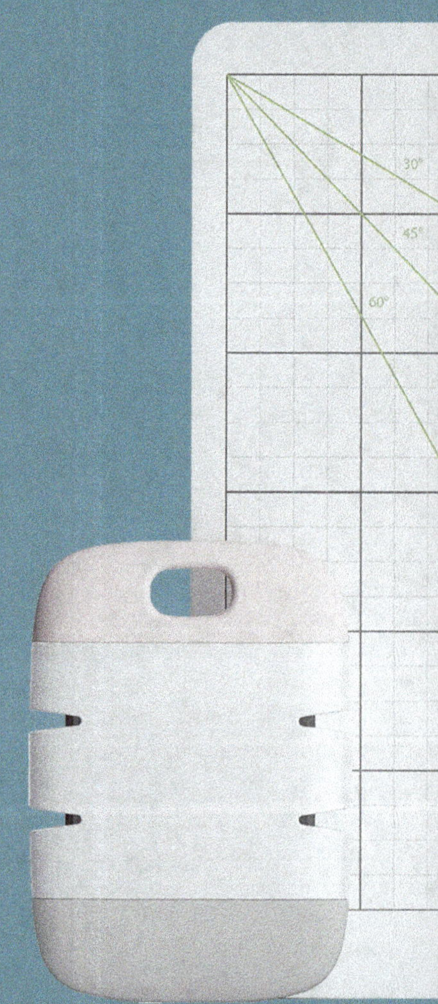

- Cricut scraper (small)
- Cricut spatula

Cricut Precision Cutting Kit

The Cricut Precision Cutting tool kit includes the following tools:
- Cricut TrueControl knife
- Cricut TrueControl blades (x 5)
- Cricut blade storage cartridge
- Cricut 18" x 24" ruler
- Cricut 12" x 12" self-healing crafting mat

Cricut Paper Tool Kit

The Cricut Paper tool kit includes the following tools:
- Cricut piercer
- Cricut quilting tool
- Cricut edge distresser
- Cricut 5" x 6" self-healing crafting mat

Cricut Essential Tool Kit

The Cricut Essential tool kit includes the following tools:
- Cricut Fine Point tweezer
- Cricut classic weeding tool

- Cricut spatula
- Cricut portable trimmer
- Cricut scraper (small)
- Cricut 5″ scissors for crafting
- Cricut Stylus scoring pen

Cricut Weeding/Vinyl Tool Kit

The Cricut Weeding/Vinyl tool kit includes the following tools:

- Cricut piercer
- Cricut quilting tool
- Cricut edge distresser
- Cricut 5″ x 6″ self-healing crafting mat

Cricut Scraper and Spatula Kit

The Cricut Paper tool kit includes the following tools:

- Cricut scraper (small)
- Cricut spatula

Cricut Brayer and Remover Tool Kit

The Cricut Brayer and Remover tool kit includes the following tools:

- Cricut brayer tool

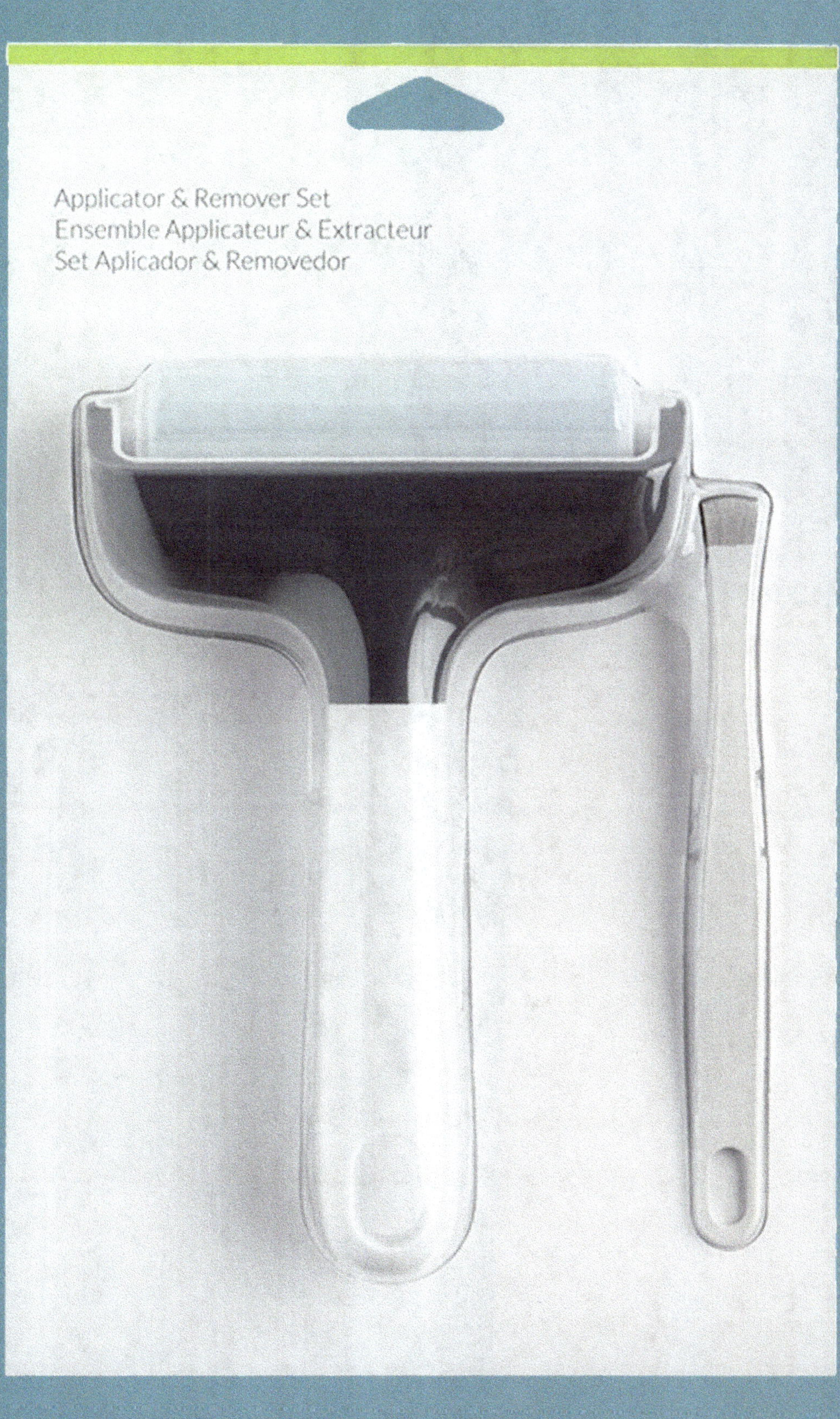

Applicator & Remover Set
Ensemble Applicateur & Extracteur
Set Aplicador & Removedor

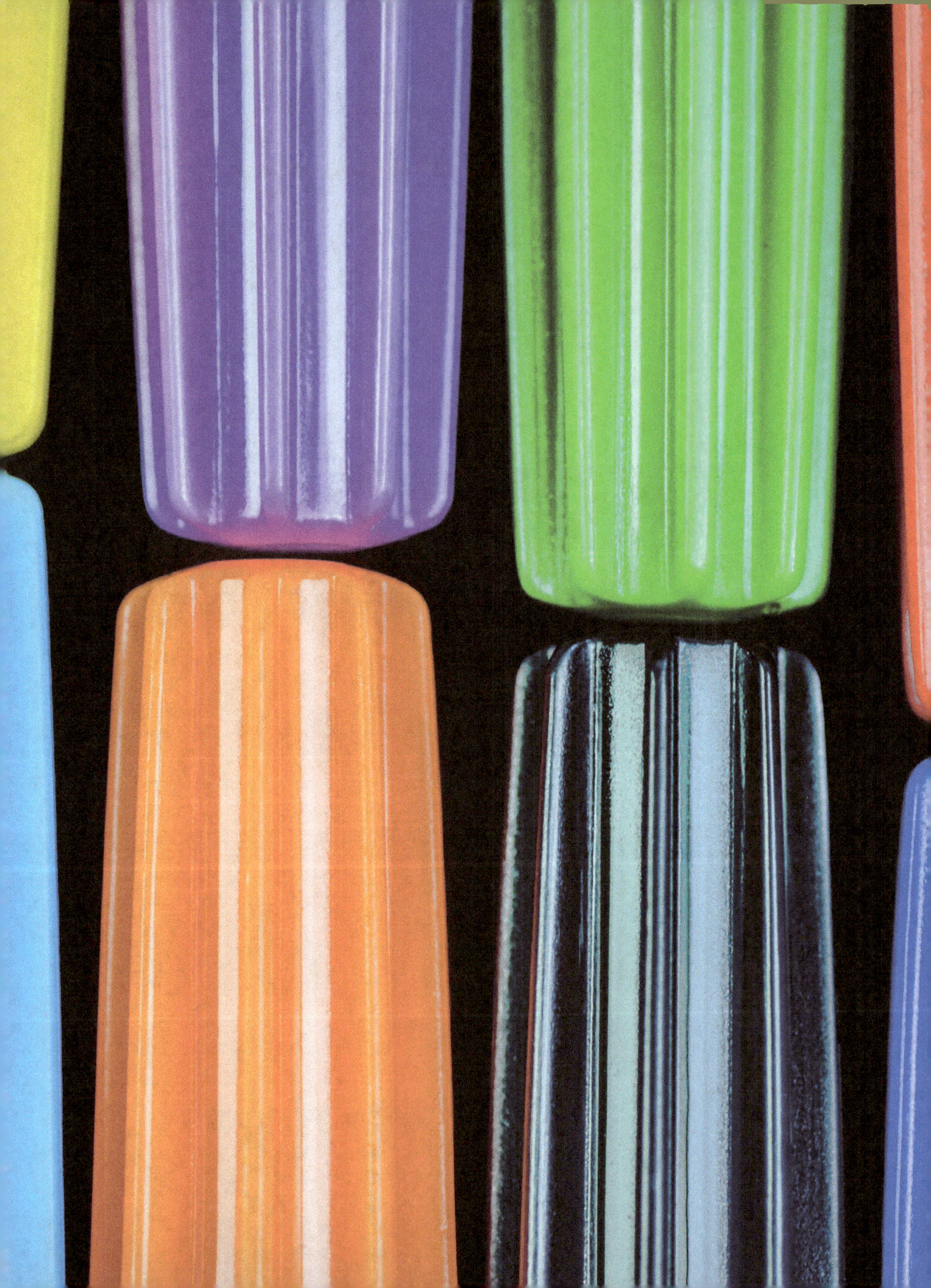

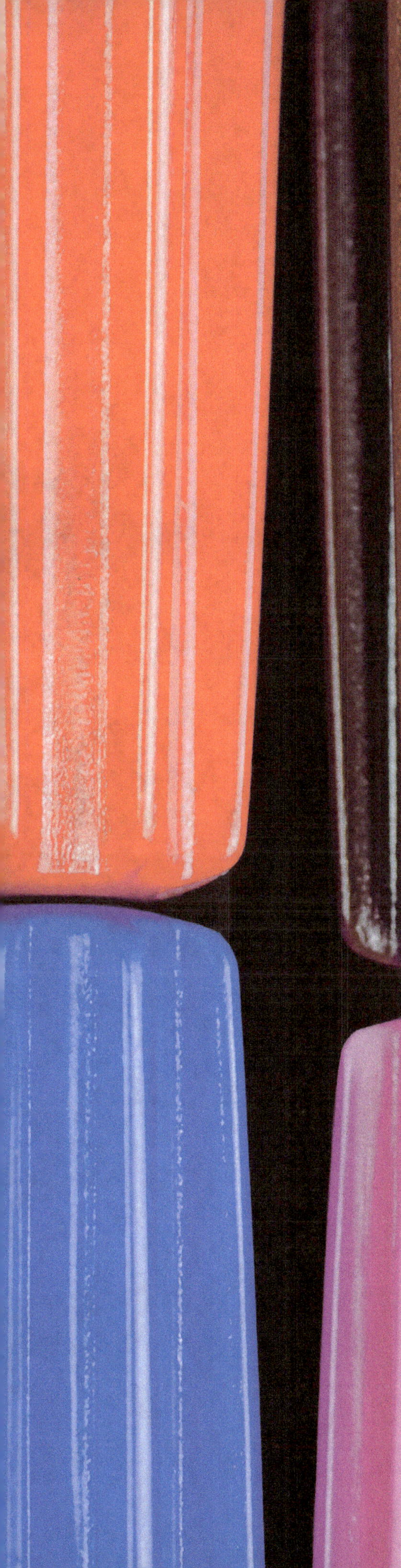

- Cricut Broadtip tweezers

Cricut Rotary Cutting Kit

The Cricut Rotary Cutting tool kit includes the following tools:

- Cricut rotary cutter (45mm)
- Cricut 12" x 24" acrylic ruler (oversized)
- Cricut 18" x 24" self-healing double-sided crafting mat

Cricut TrueControl Knife Kit

The Cricut TrueControl Knife tool kit includes the following tools:

- Cricut TrueControl knife
- Cricut TrueControl blades (x 5)
- Cricut blade storage cartridge

Cricut Pens

There are two types of Cricut craft pens; the freehand pens and the infusible ink pens. They come in different colors and sizes. Not all pens work with all Cricut machines.
Cricut Explore One Pen
The Cricut Explore One pens come with the

Pen Accessory Adapter, which can be used with the Stylus scoring pen.

Cricut Explore One Pens Are Compatible With:

·	Cricut Explore One

·	Cricut Explore One Pens Are Not Compatible With:

·	Any other Cricut machines

Cricut Ultimate Gel Pens

The Cricut ultimate gel pens come in different colors and pen sizes.

Cricut Ultimate Gel Pens Are Compatible With:

·	Cricut Maker

·	Cricut Explore Air family

·	Cricut Explore One (these pens require an adapter for the Explore One)

·	Cricut Ultimate Gel Pens Are Not Compatible With:

·	Older Cricut machines

·	Cricut Joy

Cricut Extra Fine Point Pens

The Cricut Extra Fine Point pens come in different colors and pen sizes.

Cricut Extra Fine Point Pens Are Compatible With:

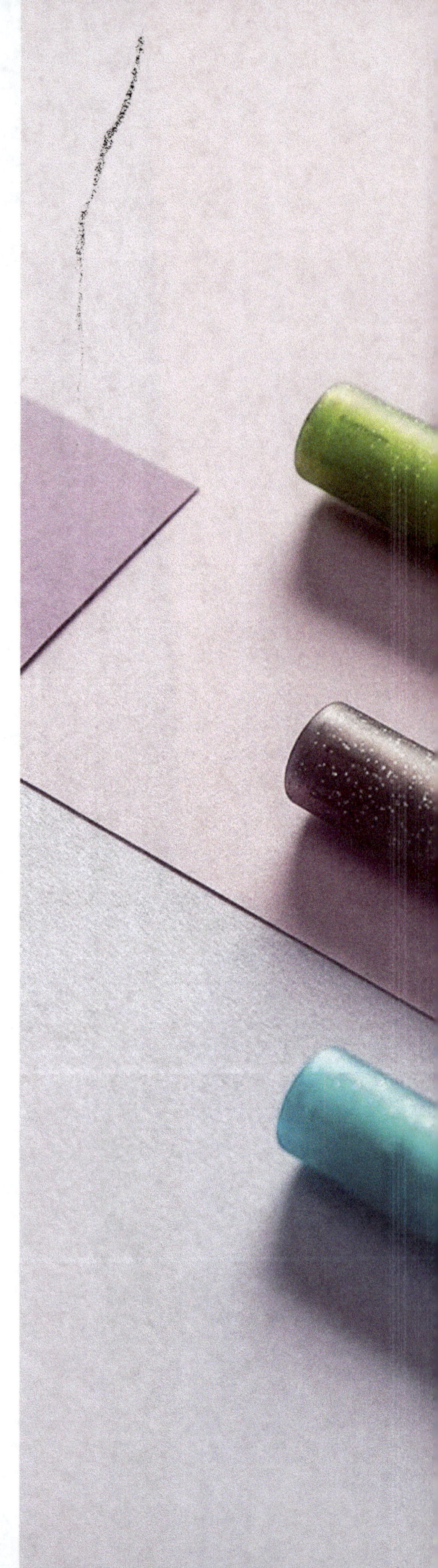

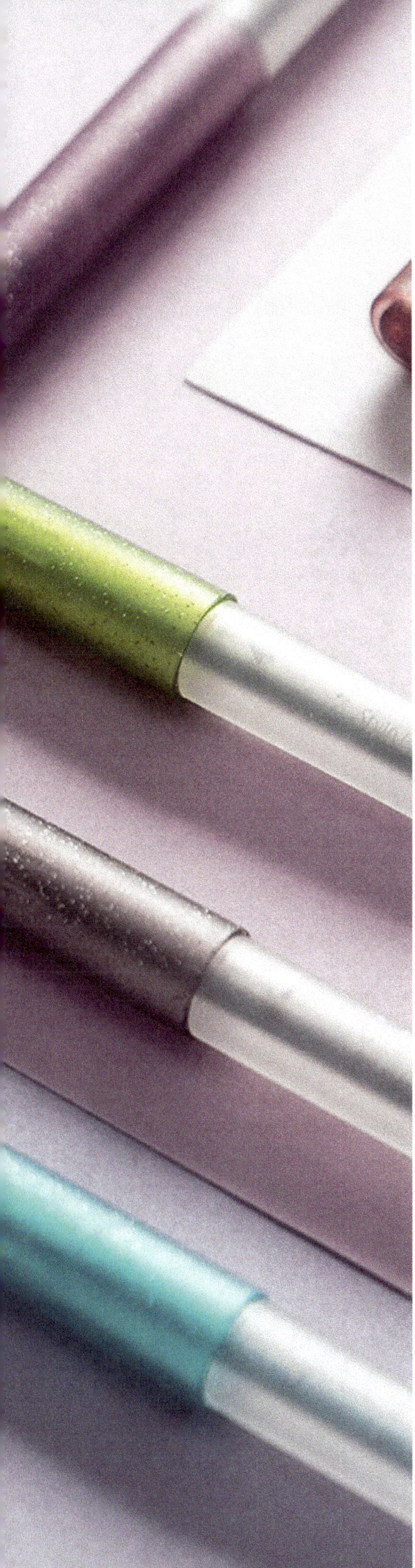

- Cricut Maker
- Cricut Explore Air family
- Cricut Explore One (these pens require an adapter for the Explore One)
- Cricut Extra Fine Point Pens Are Not Compatible With:
- Older Cricut machines
- Cricut Joy

Cricut Milky Gel Pens

The Cricut Milky Gel pens come in different colors and pen sizes.
Cricut Milky Gel Pens Are Compatible With:
- Cricut Maker
- Cricut Explore Air family
- Cricut Explore One (these pens require an adapter for the Explore One)
- Cricut Milky Gel Pens Are Not Compatible With:
- Older Cricut machines
- Cricut Joy

Cricut Glitter Gel Pens

The Cricut Glitter Gel pens come in different colors and pen sizes.
Cricut Glitter Gel Pens Are Compatible With:
- Cricut Maker
- Cricut Explore Air family

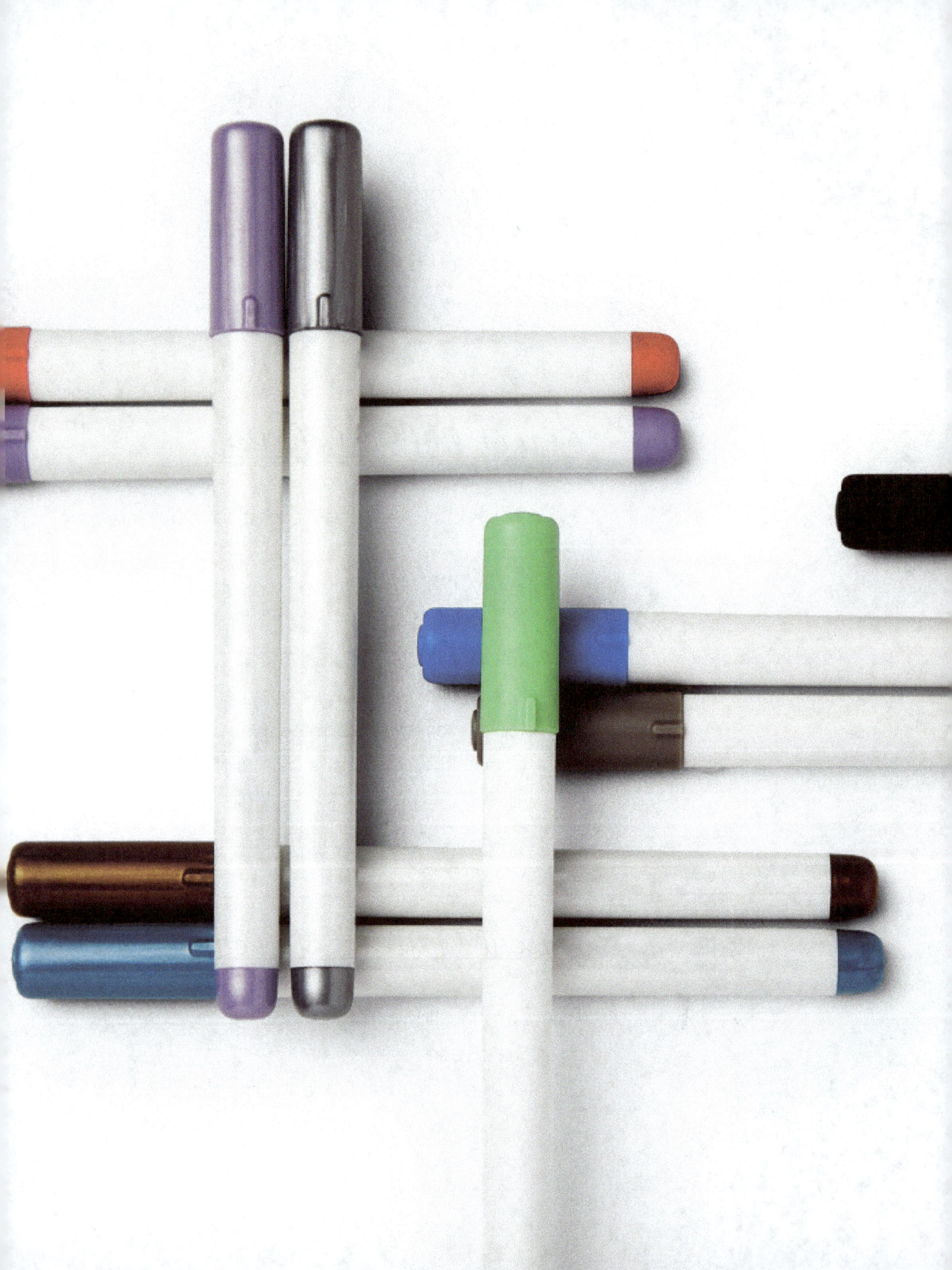

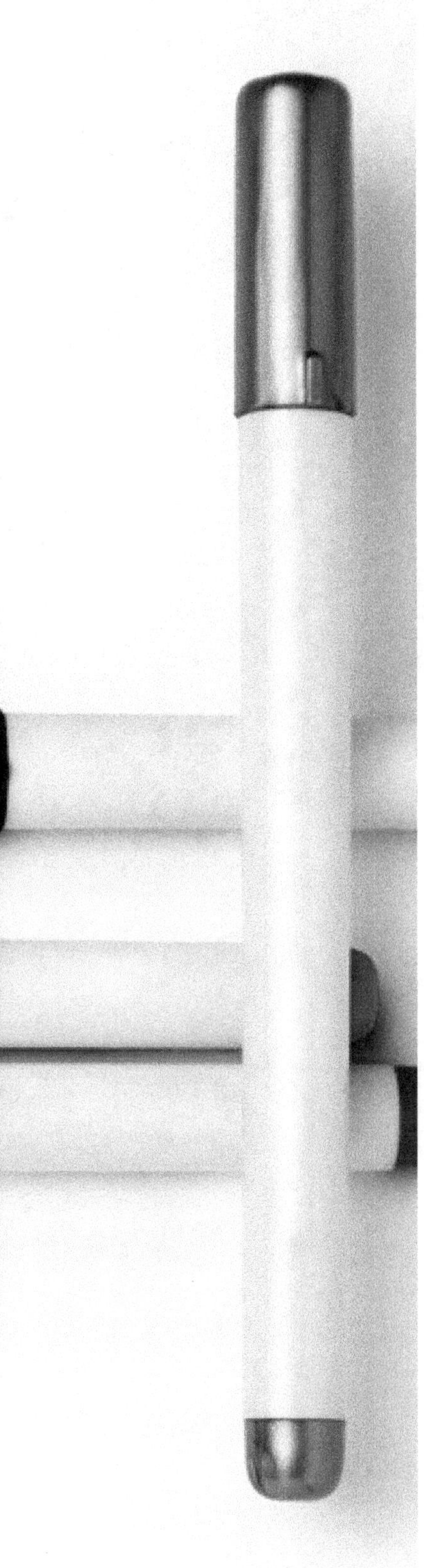

- Cricut Explore One (these pens require an adapter for the Explore One)
- Cricut Glitter Gel Pens Are Not Compatible With:
- Cricut Joy

Cricut Infusible Ink Freehand Markers Pens

The Cricut Infusible Ink Freehand marker pens come in watercolors and normal marker pens. They come in different colors and pen sizes. Cricut Infusible Ink Freehand Markers Pens Are Compatible With:
- EasyPress
- EasyPress 2
- EasyPress Mini
- Cricut Infusible Ink Freehand Marker Pens Are Not Compatible With:
- These pens cannot be used with any Cricut cutting machine

Cricut Joy Pens

The following pens are not compatible with any of the other Cricut cutting machines. These pens are only for use with the Cricut Joy:
- Cricut Joy Infusible Ink Pens in different colors and point sizes
- Cricut Joy Gel Pens in different colors and point sizes

- Cricut Joy Glitter Gel Pens in different colors and sizes
- Cricut Joy Metallic Markers in different colors and sizes
- Cricut Joy Extra Fine Point Pens in different colors

Cricut Craft Mats

Cricut has self-healing craft mats designed specifically for crafting. It must be noted that these mats are NOT for use as cutting mats. They are purely for cutting and working with material out of the cutting machine(s).

They are called self-healing mats because they close up when you cut through them. The Cricut mats have twice the self-healing power than most self-healing craft mats on the market.

These mats come double-sided with useful gridlines, numbers, and angles for 30°, 60°, and 90° angle markings on them. These craft mats come in an array of colors. Depending on the type and style of the mat, colors may include:

- Rose
- Lilac
- Blue
- Mint
- Gray
- Patterned

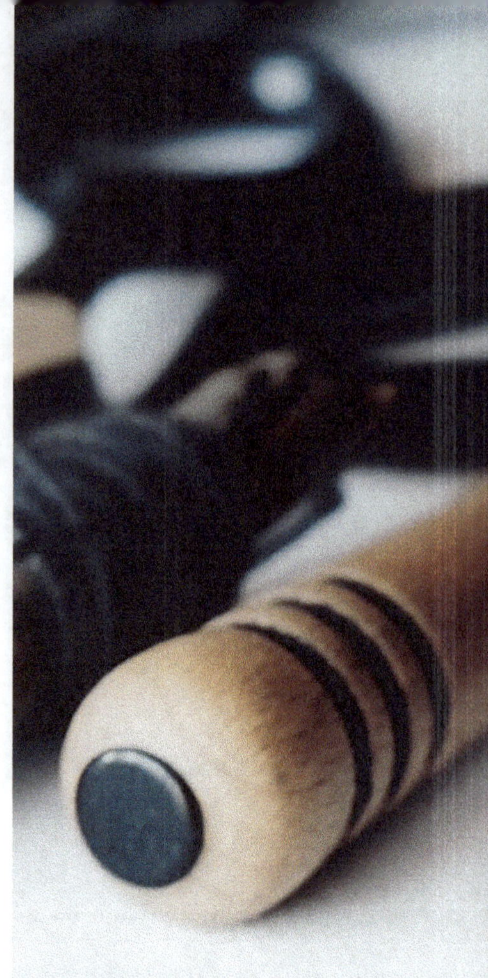

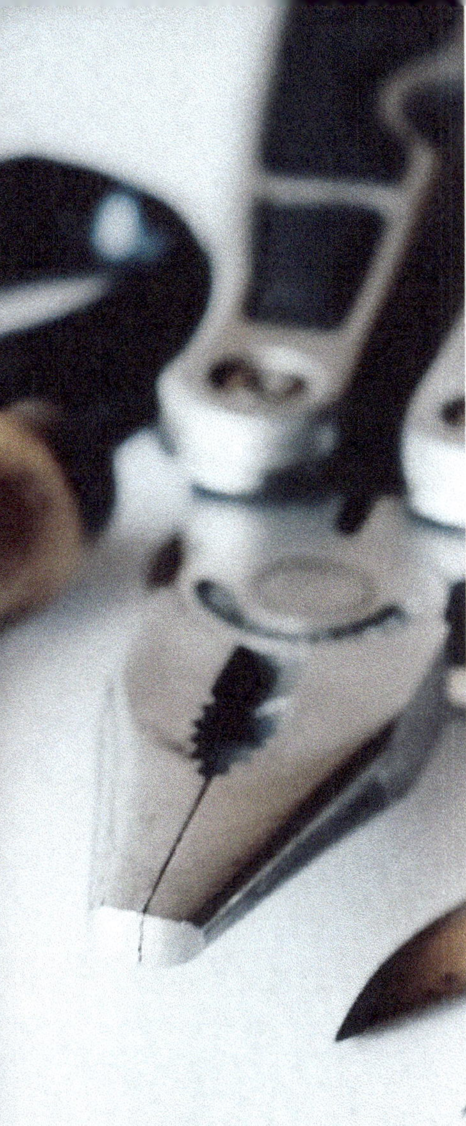

- Black

The self-healing mats come in sizes that include:

- 12" x 12."
- " x 24."
- 24" x 36."

As they are not used in a Cricut cutting machine, you can buy these mats for use with your crafts no matter which cutting machine you have.

Cricut Cutting Mats

All of the latest Cricut cutting machines, except for the Cricut Joy, use cutting mats to cut material. Four standard mats are used in these machines. The Cricut Joy does not need carpets for some cuts, but there are cuts that require a cutting mat. The Cricut Joy needs unique rugs due to their size and is not compatible with the standard mats used by other Cricut cutting machines.

Standard Cricut Cutting Mats

There are four standard Cricut cutting mats, and each rug has a different purpose and comes in one or more sizes. These mats are as follows:

- LightGrip mat – Blue
- Sizes: 12" x 12", 12" x 24", and 6" x 12"
- Material Weight: Lightweight materials
- Materials: Washi tape sheets, wrapping pa-

per, thin cardstock, printer paper, vellum, and scrapbook paper (thin sheets)
StandardGrip mat - Green
Sizes: 12″ x 12″, 12″ x 24″, and 6″ x 12″
Material Weight: Medium weight materials
Materials: Cardstock, textured paper, embossed cardstock, vinyl, and iron-on vinyl
StrongGrip mat - Purple   Sizes: 12″ x 12″, 12″ x 24″, and 6″ x 12.″
Material Weight: Heavyweight materials
Materials: Poster boards, faux leather, faux suede, corrugated cardboard, chipboard, metal, stiff fabrics, leather, thick cardstock, glitter cardstock, and mosaic vinyl.
FabricGrip mat - Pink
Sizes: Sizes: 12″ x 12″, 12″ x 24″, and 6″ x 12″
Material Weight: Fabrics as well as layered fabrics
Materials: Fabric

Cricut Joy Cutting Mats

The Cricut Joy has specific cutting mats that do not work with any other Cricut cutting machines. It should be noted that none of the standard cutting mats work with the Cricut Joy.
The Cricut Joy cutting mats include the following mats:
Cricut Joy Card Mat - Blue
Sizes: 4.5″ x 6.25.″

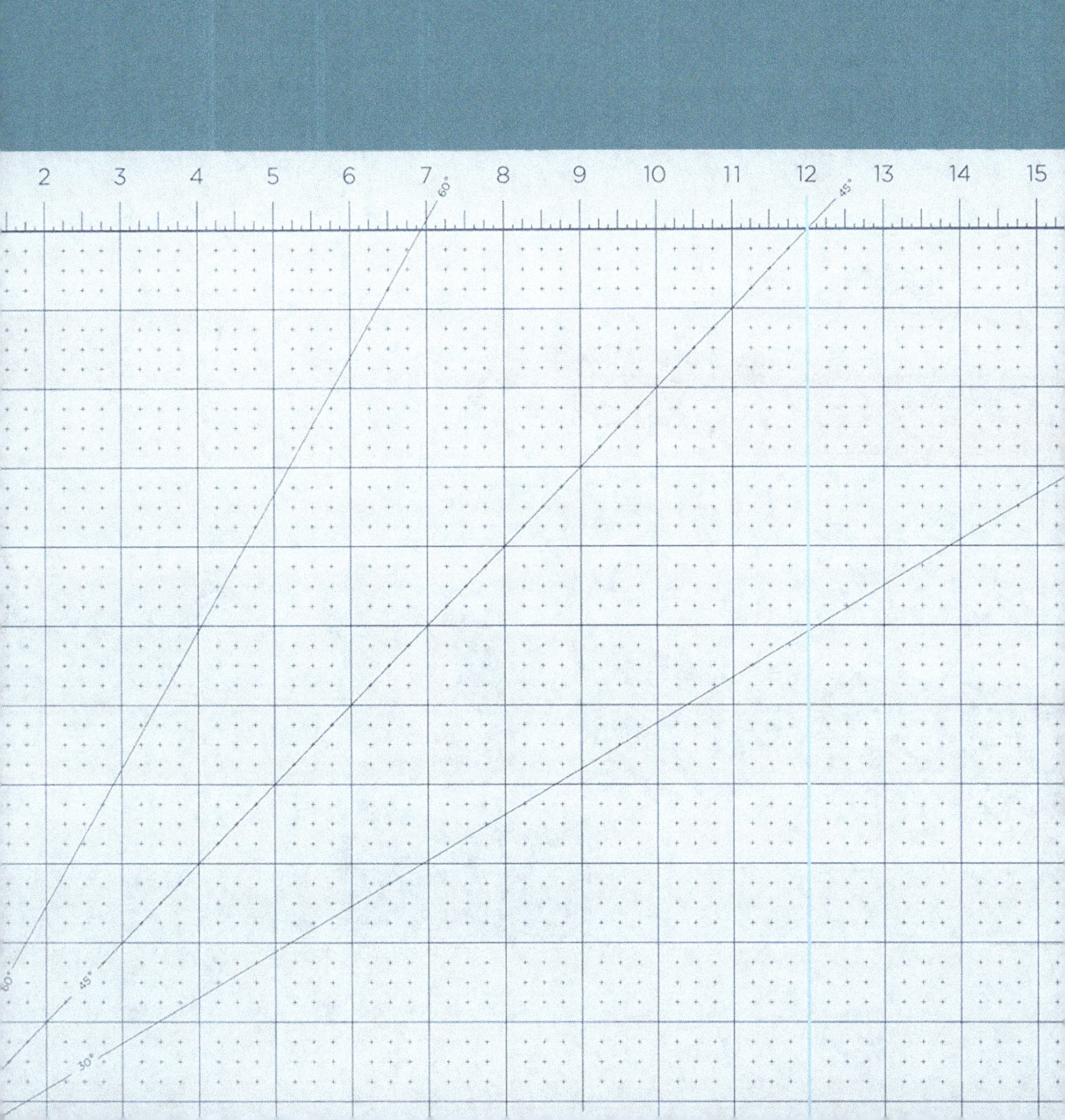

2 3 4 5 6 7 8 9 10 11 12 13 14 15
60°
45°
60°
45°
30°

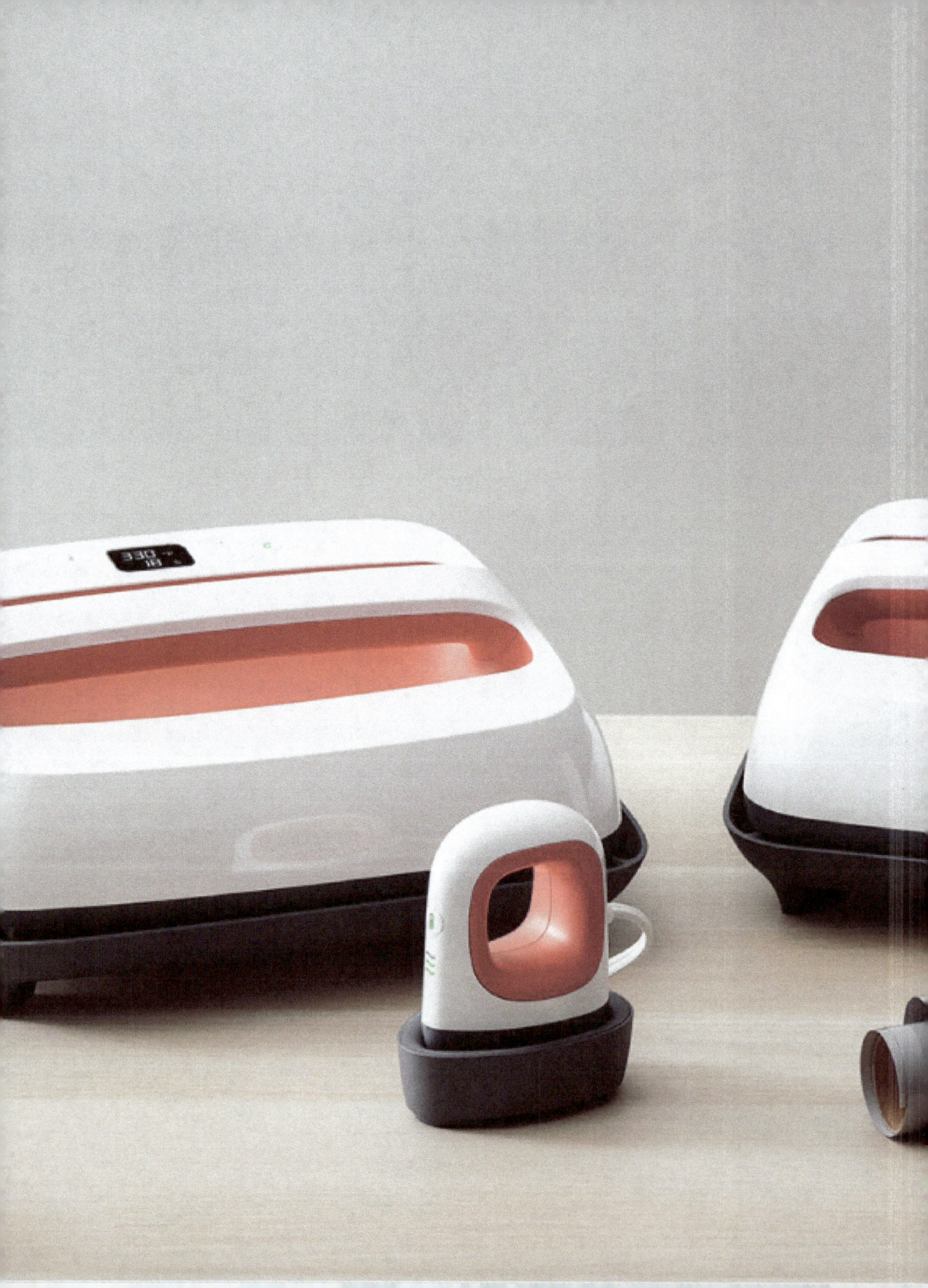

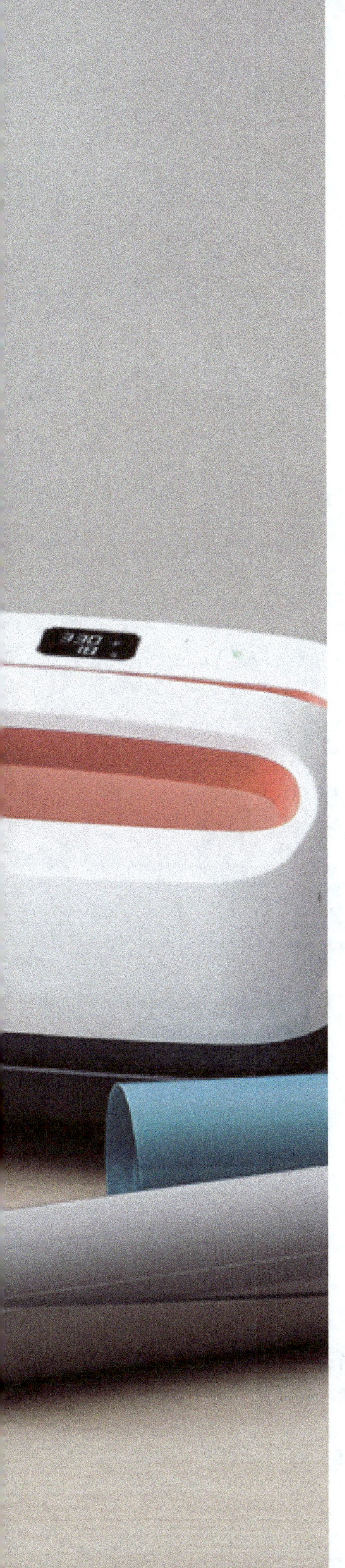

Materials: Cardstock, paper, and materials to make greeting cards
· Cricut Joy StandardGrip Mat - Green
· Sizes: 4.5" x 12" and 4.5" x 6.5."
· Material Weight: Medium weight materials
· Materials: Cardstock, textured paper, embossed cardstock, vinyl, and iron-on vinyl
· Cricut Joy LightGrip Mat - Blue
· Sizes: 4.5" x 12" and 4.5" x 6.5."
· Material Weight: Lightweight materials
· Materials: Cardstock, paper, and other lightweight materials

Cricut EasyPress Mats

For heat transfers, the EasyPress Mats are the better option to choose over an ironing board. Even if you do not have the EasyPress or one of the new EasyPresses, you should invest in one of these mats if you are crafting and using iron-on or heat transfers. Their flat, durable surface makes getting the transfer on correctly a lot easier than a conventional ironing board.

The Cricut EasyPress mats come in 4 sizes and are compatible with all EasyPress irons and mini irons.

Easy Press Mat Sizes:

- Extra-large sized mat - 20" x 16."
- Large-sized mat - 14" x 14."
- Medium-sized mat - 12" x 12."
- Small-sized mat - 8" x 10."

Cricut Access

Cricut Access is the software that gives you access to images, fonts, and the like. You will need to purchase this if you plan on using your Cricut machine, period, and if you don't have the software already, you suggest purchasing it.

The monthly option is perfect for beginners and offers over 400 different fonts and 90,000 other images. And it comes with a 10% savings on any additional Cricut purchases you need, as well as a 10% savings on premium images and fonts, such as Disney fonts. You'll also have access to a priority member line.

The next membership option is annual, precisely the same as the basic, but you don't have to pay as much - just $7.99 per month, up front. It's okay if you're serious about getting into Cricut.

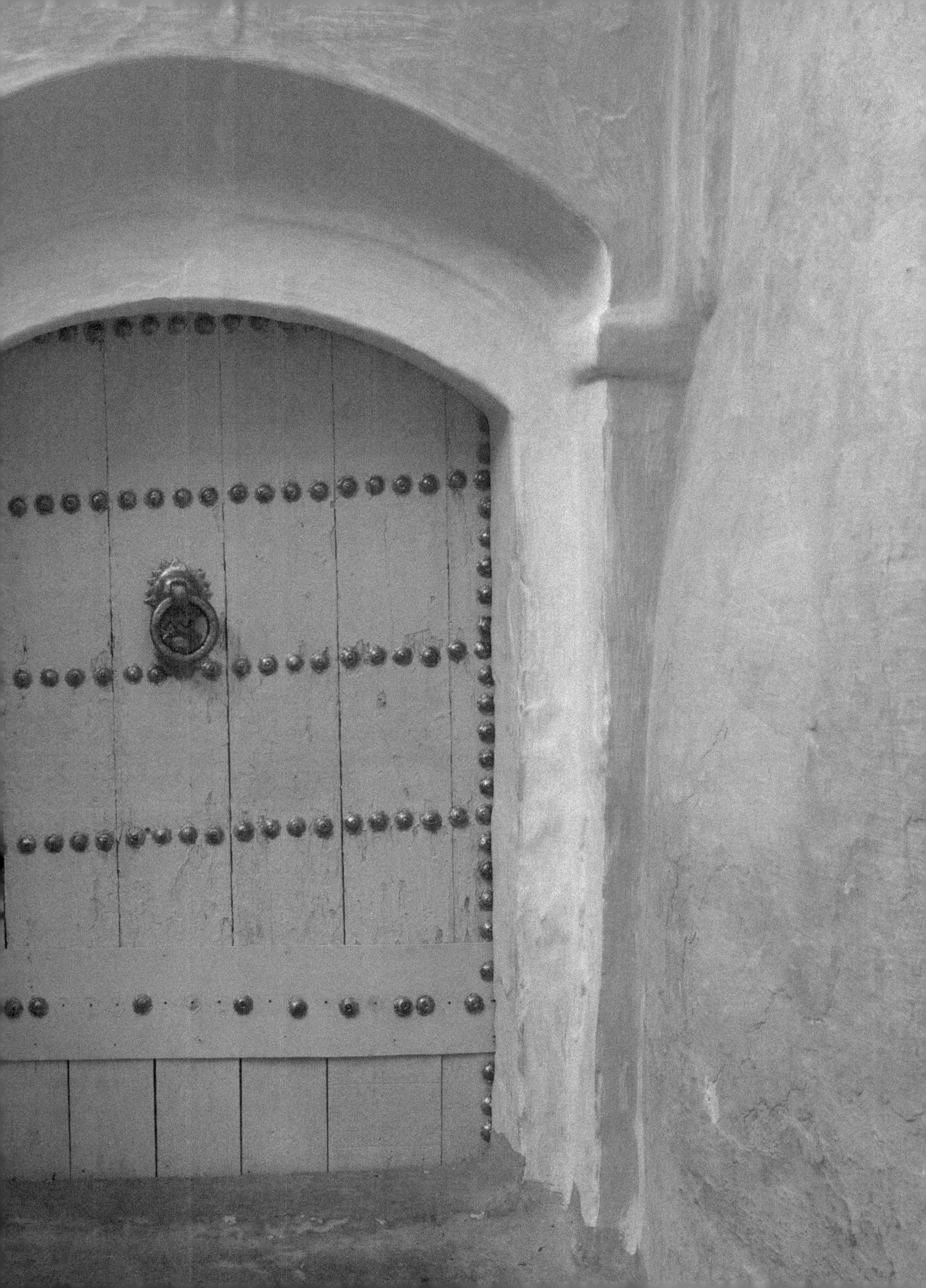

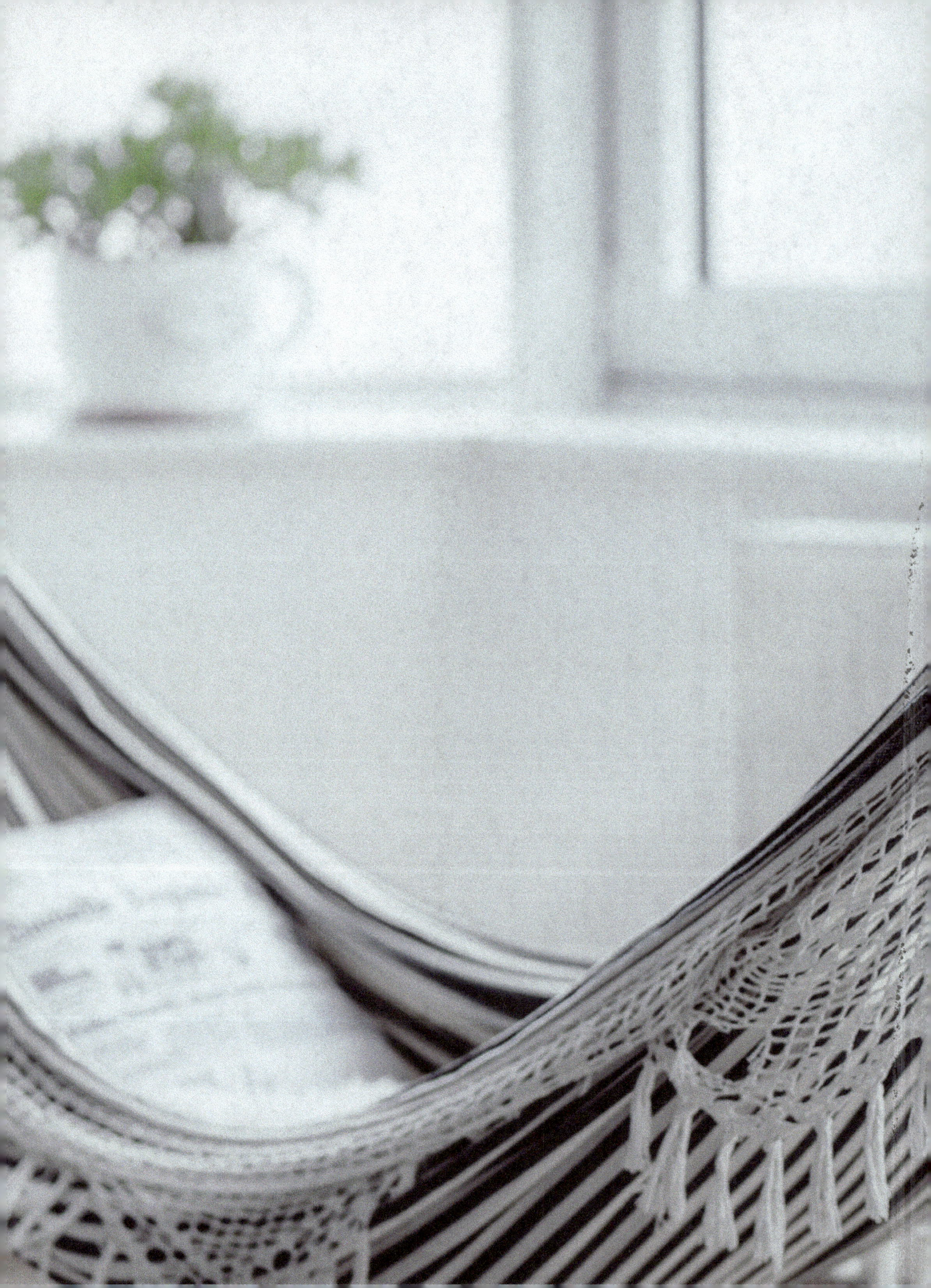

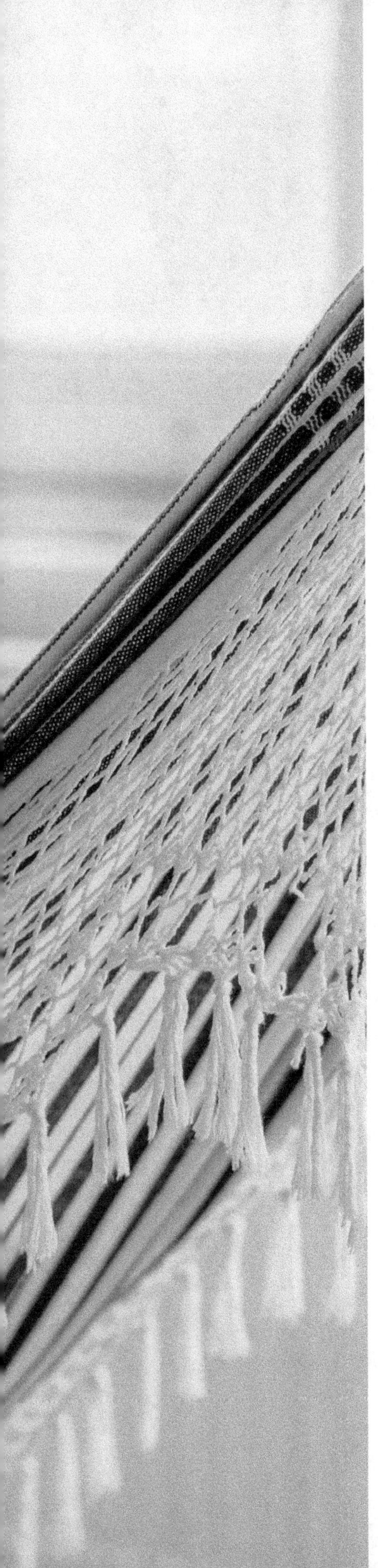

Finally, you have the premium option, which is the same price as monthly and offers unlimited access to the same fonts and images, savings on both products and licenses, and 50 extra savings on licensed pictures and fonts, along with some ready-to-make projects. If you spend over $50 on the Cricut store, you earn free shipping. You think this is the best option if you plan on spending a lot of money on Cricut items, and you're in it for the long haul. However, if you're beginning, the monthly membership is probably a better choice because you can cancel this at any time.

Membership allows you to save a little bit on premium ideas and licensed designs - the more you make with your Cricut machine, the more you save, and you'll realize that you could save a lot fast. On average, customers say that they make up the subscription costs with the money they hold, and the coolest thing is that there is so much to choose from, you can find some beautiful designs. It is excellent if you want exclusive content.

The Cricut Scraper

The Circuit Scraper tool is essential (and a lifesaver!) when you need to rid your cutting

mat of excess negative bits. This tool typically works best with paper, such as cardstock,
but other materials can easily be scraped up
as well. Use the mat's flexibility to your ad-
vantage as you scrap the bits off the car-
pet to ensure you are not scraping up the
adhesive on the mat as well. You can also
use the Cricut Scraper as a scoreline holder,
which allows you to fold over the score-line
with a nice crisp edge. It can also be used
as a burnishing tool for Cricut transfer tape,
as it will allow seamless separation of the
transfer tape from the backing.

The Cricut Spatula

A spatula is a must-have tool for a crafter
who works with a lot of paper. Pulling the
form off of a Cricut cut mat can result in
a lot of tearing and paper curling if you
are not diligent and mindful when removing
it. The spatula is thinly designed to slip right
under the paper, allowing you to ease it off
the mat carefully. Be sure to clean it often
as it is likely to get the adhesive build-up on
it after multiple uses. It can also be used as
a scraper if your scraper tool is not readily
available!

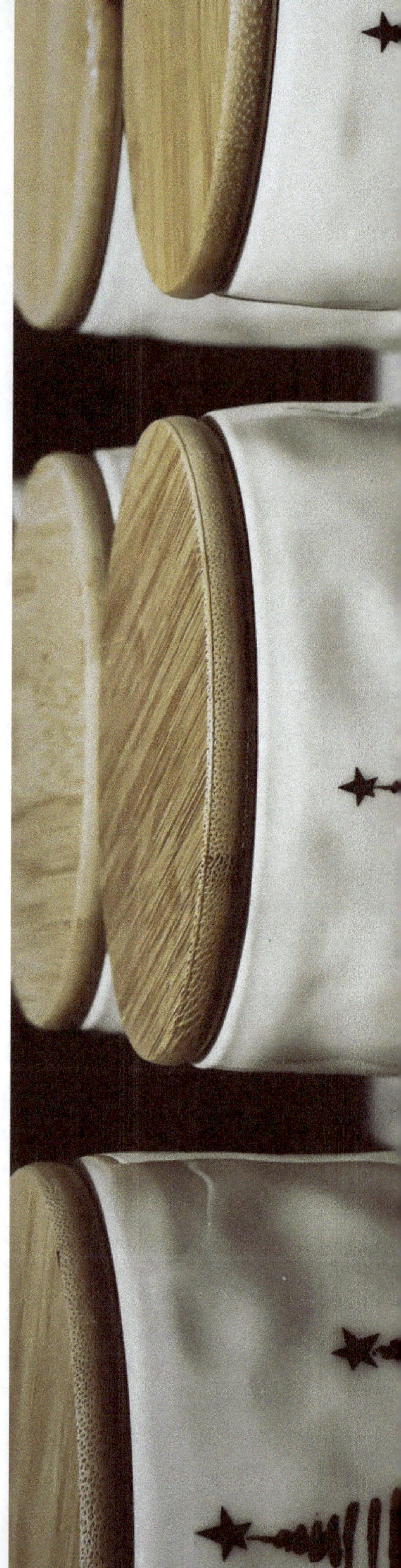

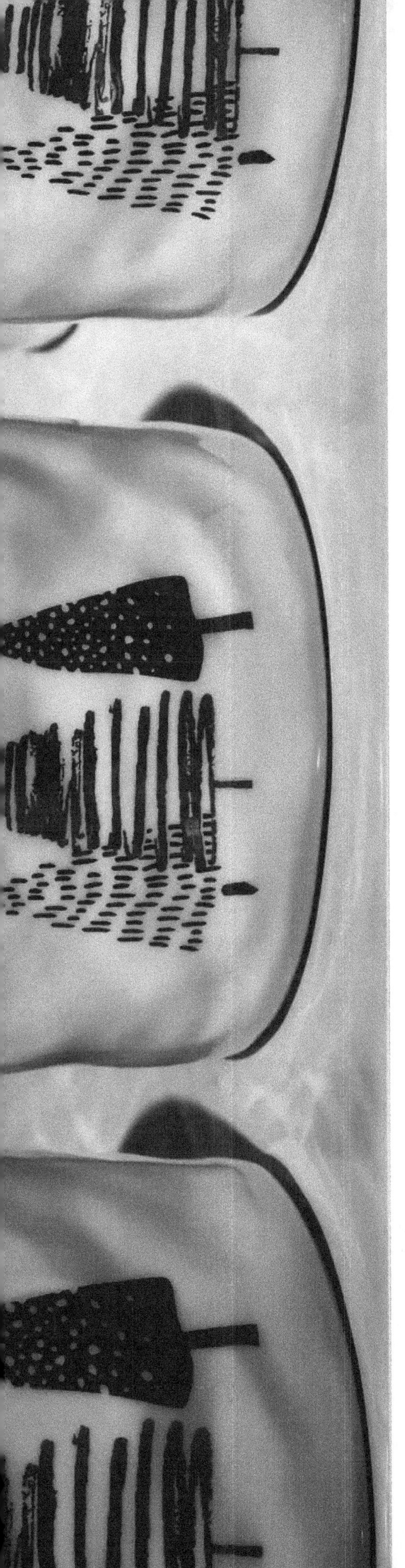

Storage

There are three different categories of storage bags specifically designed for "Cricut" machines and tools as described below:

Machine Totes

These premium storage bags are 26″ long, 9.25″ wide, and 9.25″ tall and carefully designed so you can organize and store your "Cricut" machine at home and easily transport it if needed. The bag has side pockets and compartments to store craft tools and supplies and comes with a sturdy double-snap handle. These bags have soft padding to provide additional protection and shock absorption. You can buy these bags in different colors (Purple, Navy, Tweed, and Raspberry) for $149.99.

Rolling Craft Tote

These bags are equipped with rollers for easy portability and storage at home. They are 26″ long, 10.25″ wide, and 14.38″ tall but remember these bags are designed to store your craft supplies and will not fit any "Cricut" machines. These bags are also available

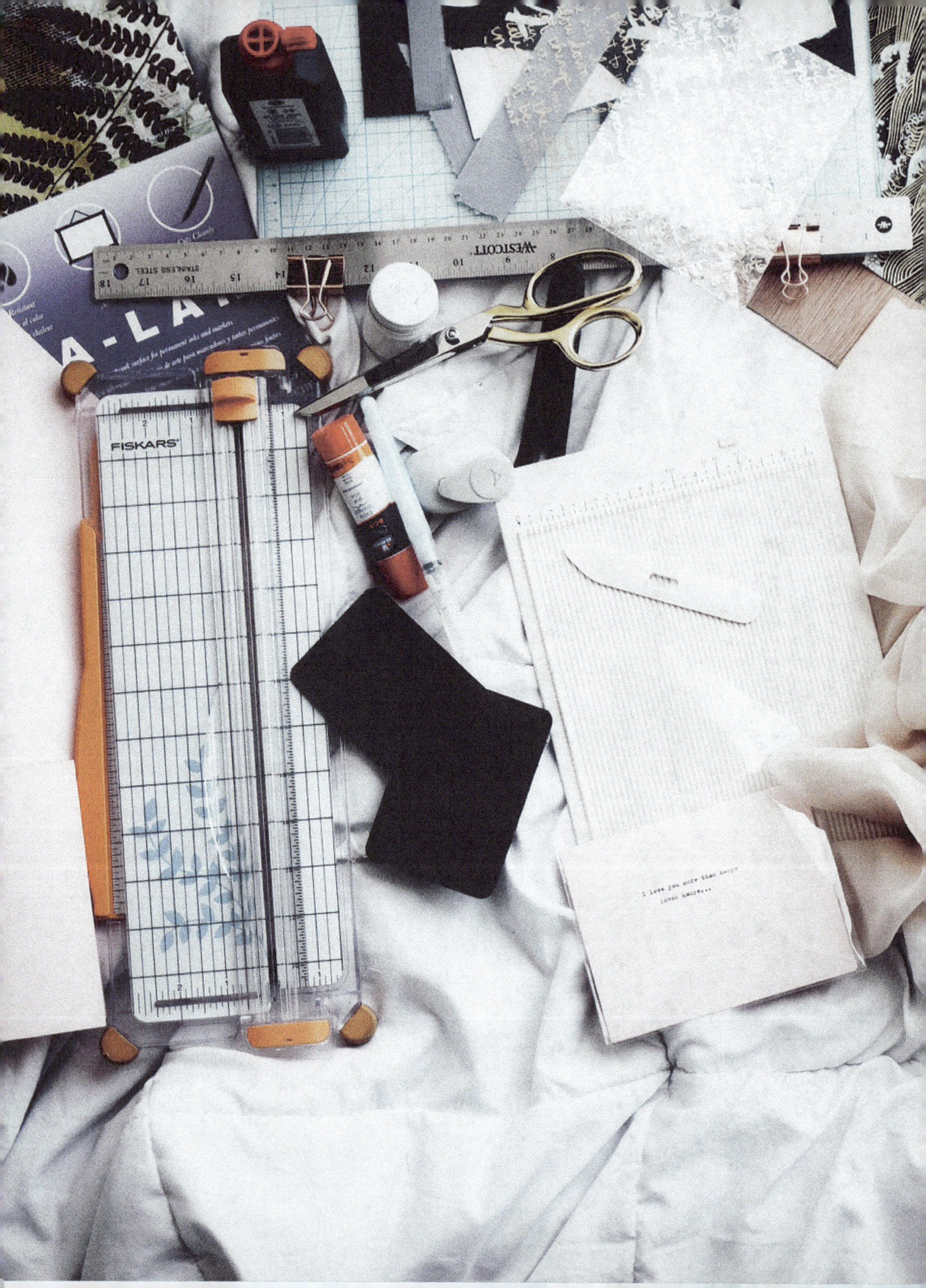

I love you more than bugs
love hugs...

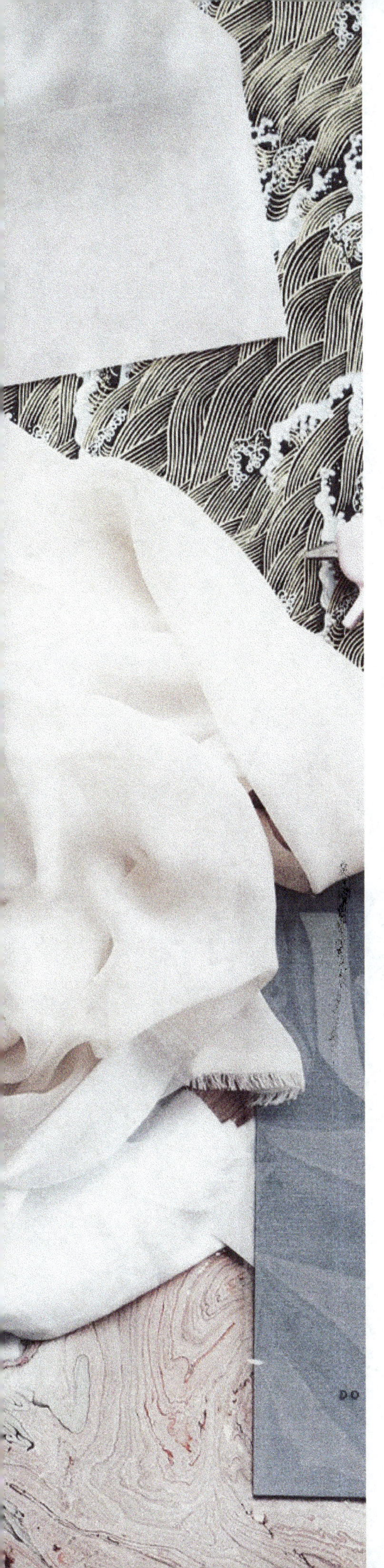

in different colors (Purple, Navy, Tweed, and Raspberry) for $199.99.

EasyPress Tote

These bags are specifically designed to store "Cricut EasyPress" along with its safety base, mat, and other small accessories at home or on the go. They are made from robust and heat-resistant material to protect your device against bumps and scratches while you work through your heat-transfer projects. A convenient shoulder strap and full gripped handle will allow for easy carrying around with the Velcro strap to secure your device for travel. A back pocket and front pocket are added to store the mats and iron-on accessories.

Techniques

Hacks, tips, and techniques-call it what you want, but every Cricut crafter needs to know them to make crafting much more comfortable, faster, and fuss-free. We will explore the many hacks regarding tools and supplies organizing, how to get the most out of your purchases, how to save time and money, and much more.

How to Organize Cricut Sup-

Making your craft space organized, no matter how big or small is imperative. First things firsts:

Cricut Mat Organization

You will have plenty of mats for various crafting needs, and the more you continue your Cricut crafts, the more carpets you'll have. So how do you keep them all organized? Hanging your mats on the wall according to the grip strength is one way. You can use basket storage or file storage, and you can even use command hooks to organize and sort your mats. Having them displayed on the wall will save you some time looking and searching for them.

Cricut Vinyl Rolls

One of the best ways to keep all your vinyl rolls perfectly organized is using Ikea trash bag holders. Crafters swear by it. Just do a quick Google search, and you'll find plenty of images showing you how you can stack these rolls easily in the

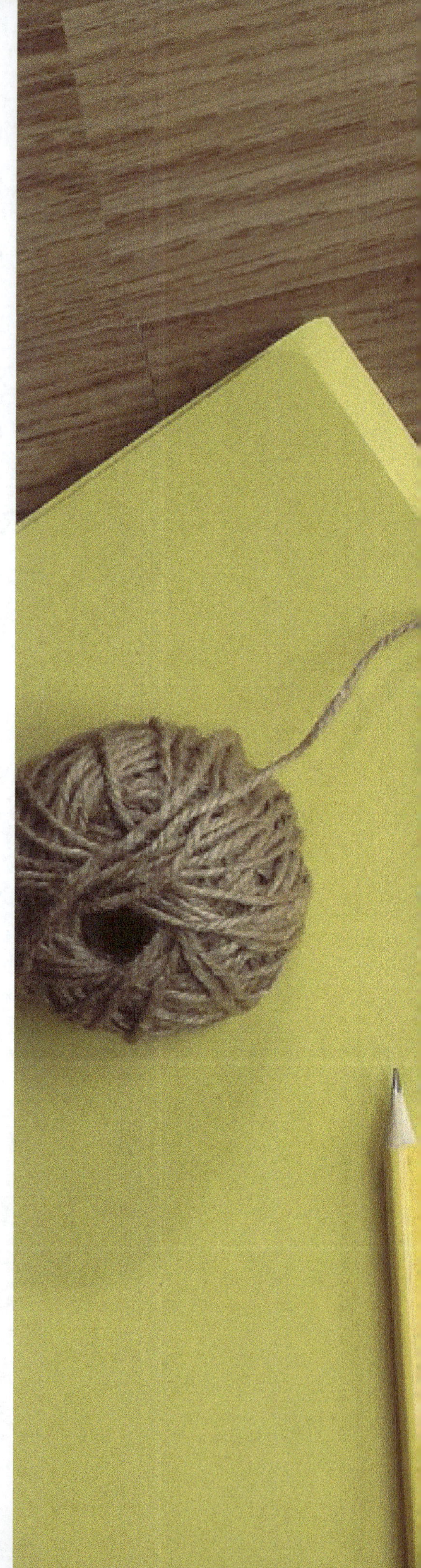

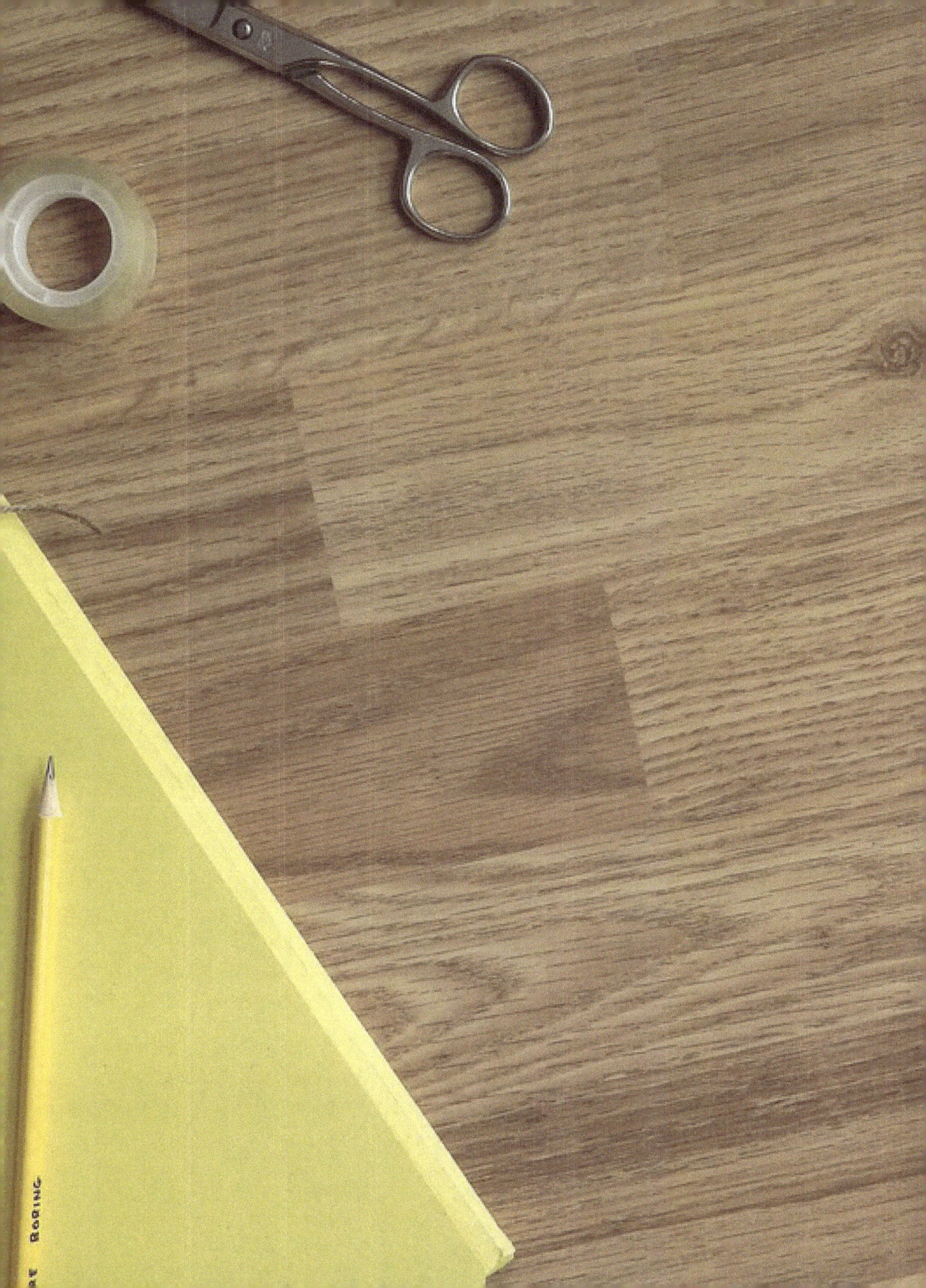

holders. The holders cost only about $10 or so, and they can hold up to 14 registrations each. Get a few of them and organize your rolls according to color and style.

Cricut tools

For tools, you can use jars or canisters to keep your devices safely and securely. Some crafters also use $5 pegboards purchased from Target with tiny holes in them that you can easily hang. Keeping them on pegboards prevents the nuisance of digging around for them. You get to see your tools displayed nicely, and there's no guessing where everything is. All your devices are within easy reach.

How to Quickly Weed Vinyl

Weeding is both satisfying and troublesome at the same time. Some crafters find joy in weeding out all the little cuts because it's very gratifying to see your artwork coming together, but it is bothersome as well because weeding out takes time.
The best way to make this process fast is by using your Cricut Bright Pad. All you need to do is place your craft on the top of the lightbox, so the light peeks throu-

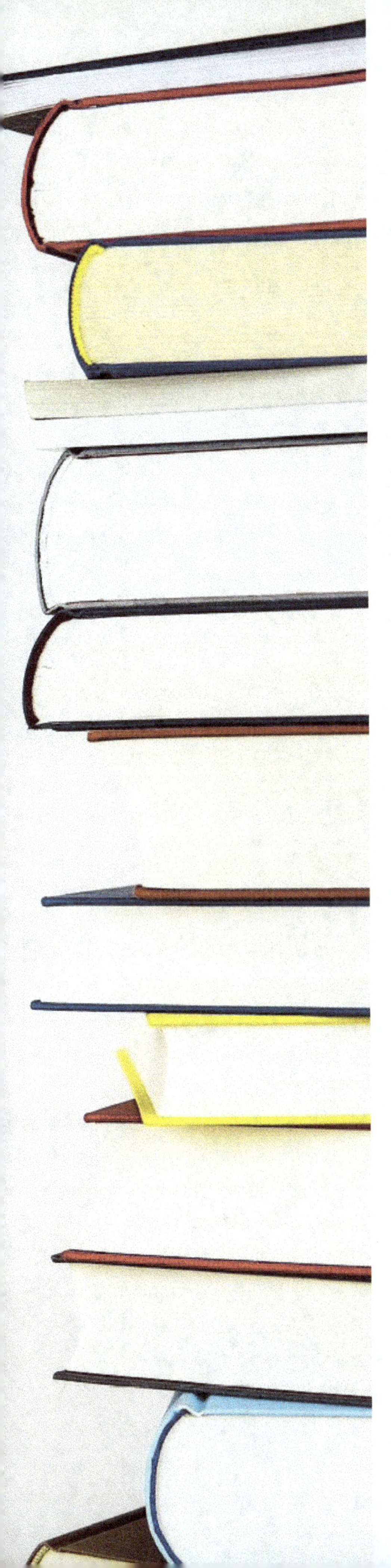

gh all those intricate cut lines. You can see all these lines more visibly, and it also saves time because you do not need to guess where the cuts are. If the BrightPad is not within your budget, you can also place your vinyl on a window or a brighter area, so the light makes it easier for you to see.

Conventional irons have hot and cold spots that result in you taking more time to cover your iron projects' surface to ensure that everything sticks on easily. The Easy Press has a large surface area, and the heating is distributed evenly on the entire body, ensuring that your iron-on is safely and securely ironed on. You do not need to worry about burning your project because the temperature is too hot on one end while the other end doesn't even stick. When working with iron-on, look at the Cricut temperature chart to select the appropriate temperature for your craft and the time needed to press until the machine beeps.

How to Use Vinyl Scraps

Many crafters do not throw away their vinyl scraps because they can be used again. Plus, it helps if you use the chips also to save the environment. One of the best ways to use scraps is to place them on your mat and use the Snap Mat feature found in the Cricut App. What this does is that it will take a photo of your mat and allows you to arrange your designs on the scraps so that they can be cut out entirely. This means no more guesswork and no more waste. These scraps also work great with quilters working on fussy cuts on their fabric. You can use the Snap Mat features to take a photo of the material and the mat. Next, place these designs over the images you want to cut out.

Cricut Explore And Maker Pen Hack

Cricut has a fantastic array of pens, and they always come up with new pen products to help you explore and enhance your creativity. Apart from using the Cricut markers, did you know that you can use any other sharpie or marker or colored pencil with your Cricut machine?

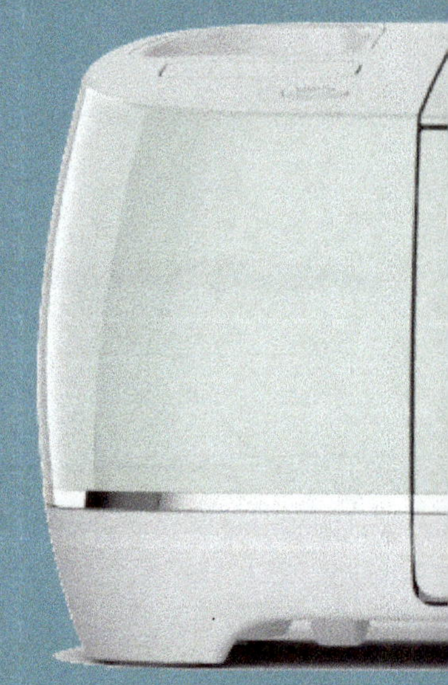

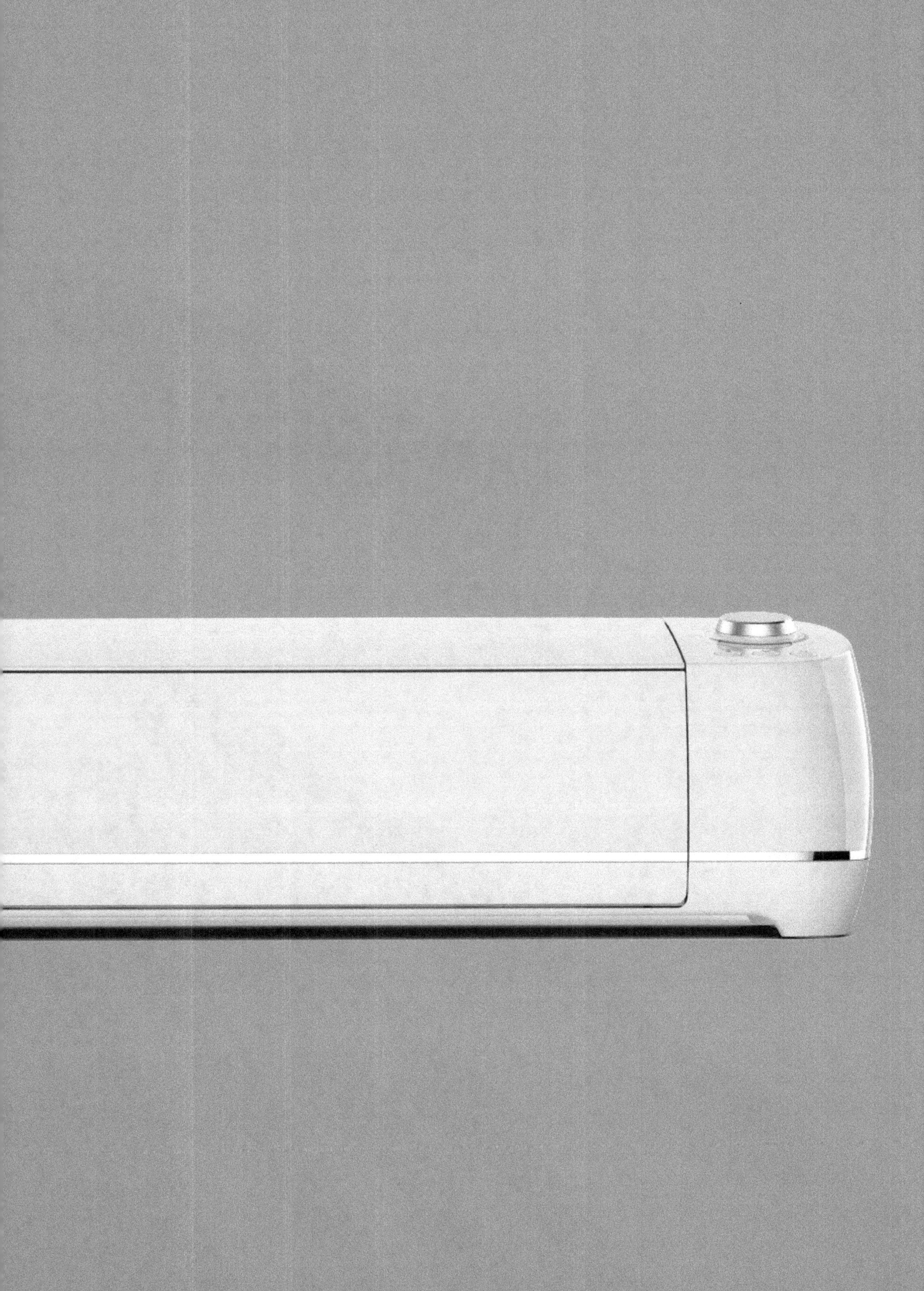

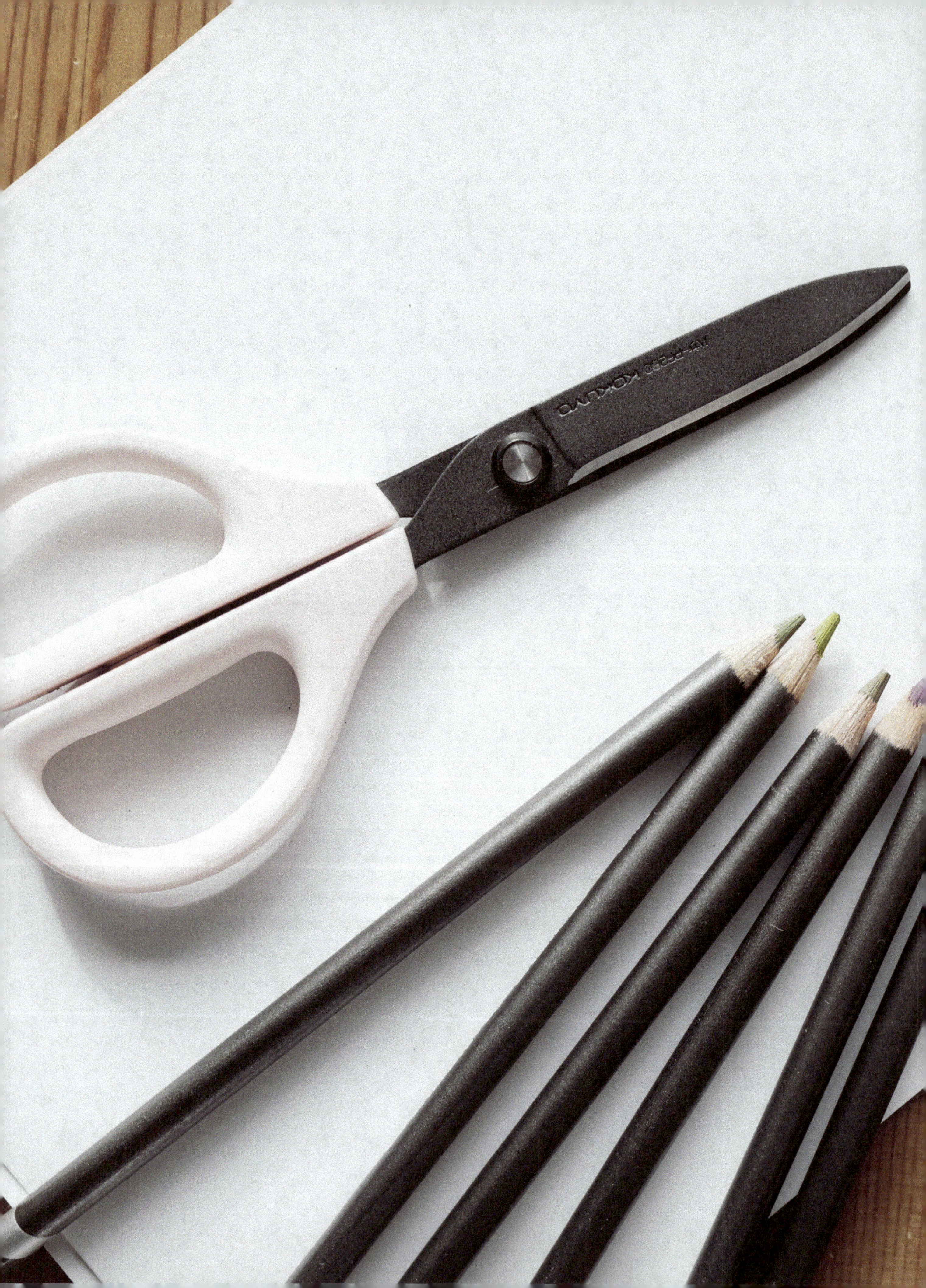

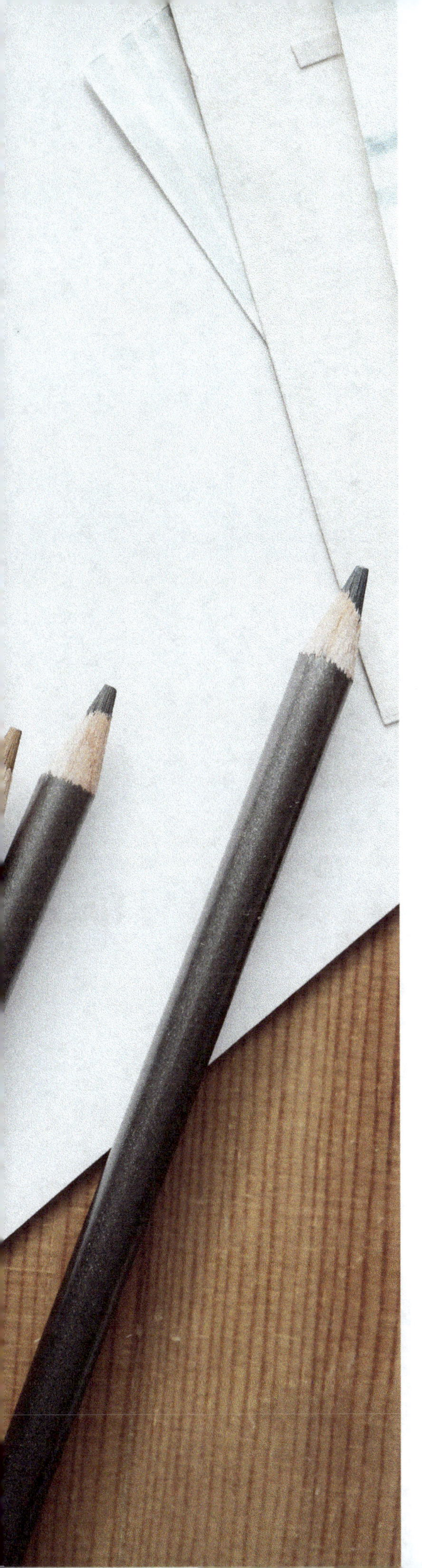

Chapter 3

How to use accessories and tools

As a Cricut user, knowing the essential tools and functions of the Cricut Design Space is necessary. Not knowing them means you can't handle even the simplest of projects on your own, which doesn't look too good. This chapter will take you through all the fundamental tools and functions on the Cricut Design Space to ensure you have the right base that can build you to attain mastery. Don't worry about using these tools and procedures now; ensure that you know how they work. This is all that learning is about; know how things work and making exploits with them. Also, the chapter will include essential tips and techniques on some of the tools and functions. This part will show you how special some of these tools and procedures are. After reading this chapter of the book, you should be eager and prepared to begin a new personal project by yourself.

Rudimentary Tools

Tools are essential in every work; you can barely make progress without them. Every field of work has its tools, so does the Design Space. Sometimes, the number of devices you use during your project can determine the beauty of your project output. There are so many tools in the Design Space, and we shall take a look at most of them and what they do.

Cricut Design Space Canvas Area

Starting with the Canvas area is that all the arts and designing happen on this platform. The Canvas area is where you will be making use of your tools the most. You can easily carry out the organizing of your projects and the uploading of fonts and images here.
The Design Space is parallel with many other designing and editing programs people use out there if you look closely. Programs such as Photoshop, Illustrator, and Adobe Creative

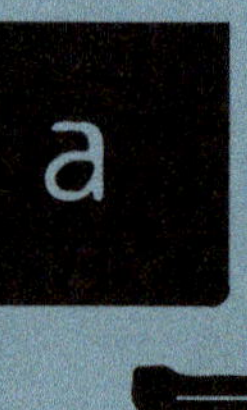

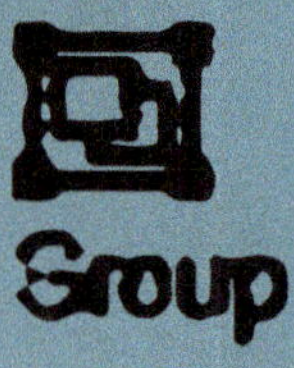

Cloud are all similar to Cricut Design Space. Therefore, if you've got prior experience using these programs, you shouldn't find it too challenging to flow with the Cricut Design Space.

As mentioned in the first chapter, getting your membership for Cricut Access activated can help you design better and enhance your creativity.

Thus, the Canvas area is where your designs can be edited and perfected before cutting them. Nonetheless, there're several options to explore when working on the Canvas area, and you might get overwhelmed easily. So, we'll be discussing these options one after another, making their uses known as we proceed.

The Canvas area consists of four panes: the right panel, left panel, top panel, and canvas area. This section will discuss the right and left panels, while the next team will discuss the top panel and canvas area.

The right panel

The Right panel is made up of layers; therefore, it's safe to call it the "Layers Panel." Layers indicate the designs present in the Canvas area. The number of layers you'll be using will depend on your project's intricacy of design.

Take a birthday card, for example; you'll have different texts and decorations on it, and possibly one or two pictures. These are called the layers of your design.

This panel enables the creation and management of layers when a design is being made. All the items on the Layer Panel will show the Line type or Fill you're using.

Group, ungroup, duplicate, and delete.

These tools enable the moving around of different designs on the Canvas area.

Group: This tool permits you to join or group different layers. When many layers need to come together to form a design, you can use the "Group" tool to bring everything together. For instance, if you are designing a house or building, there'll be diverse parts and sections in that building. A typical

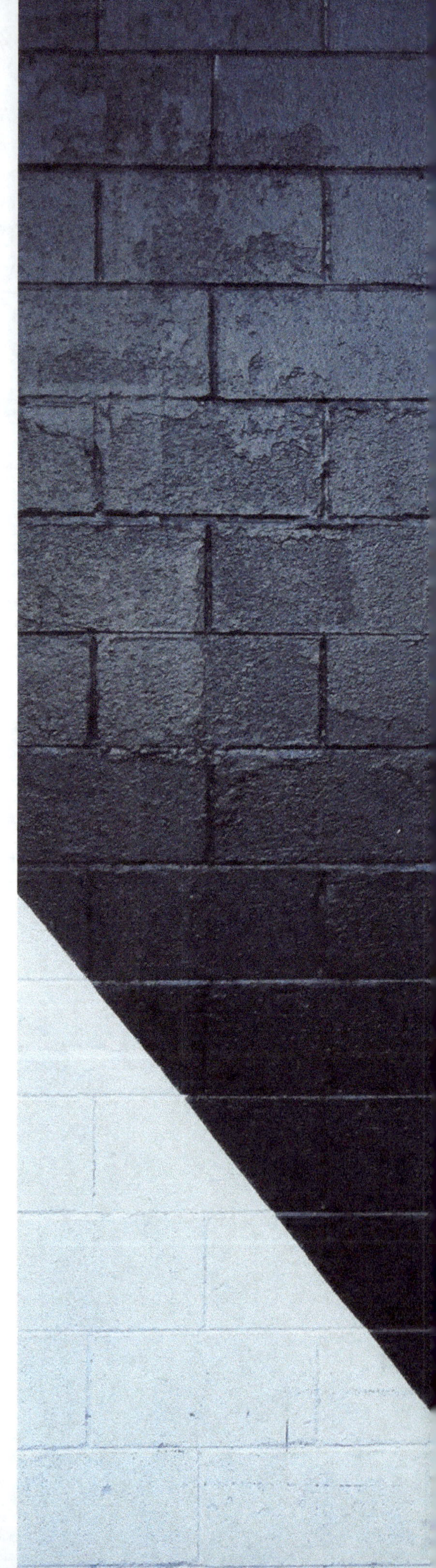

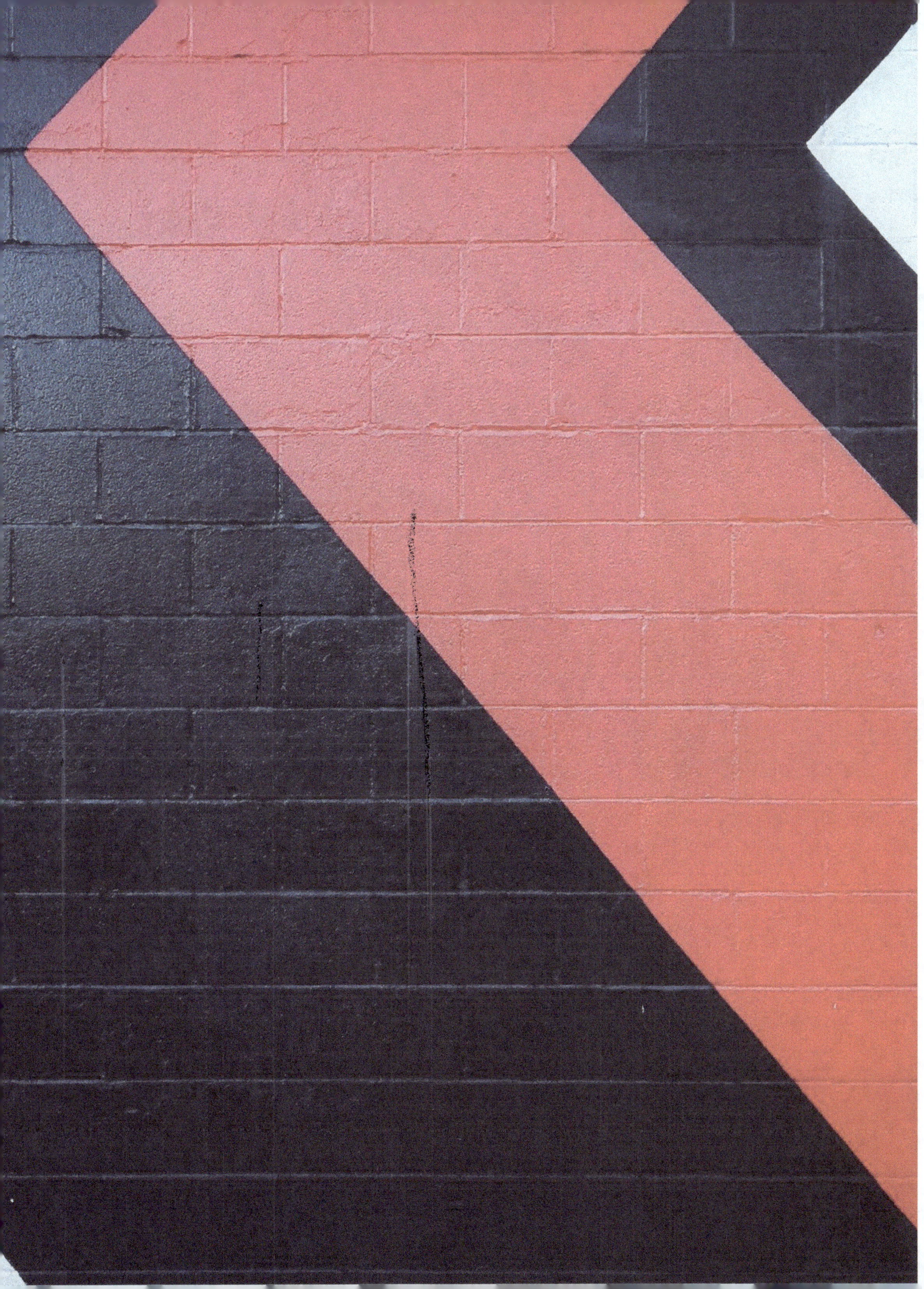

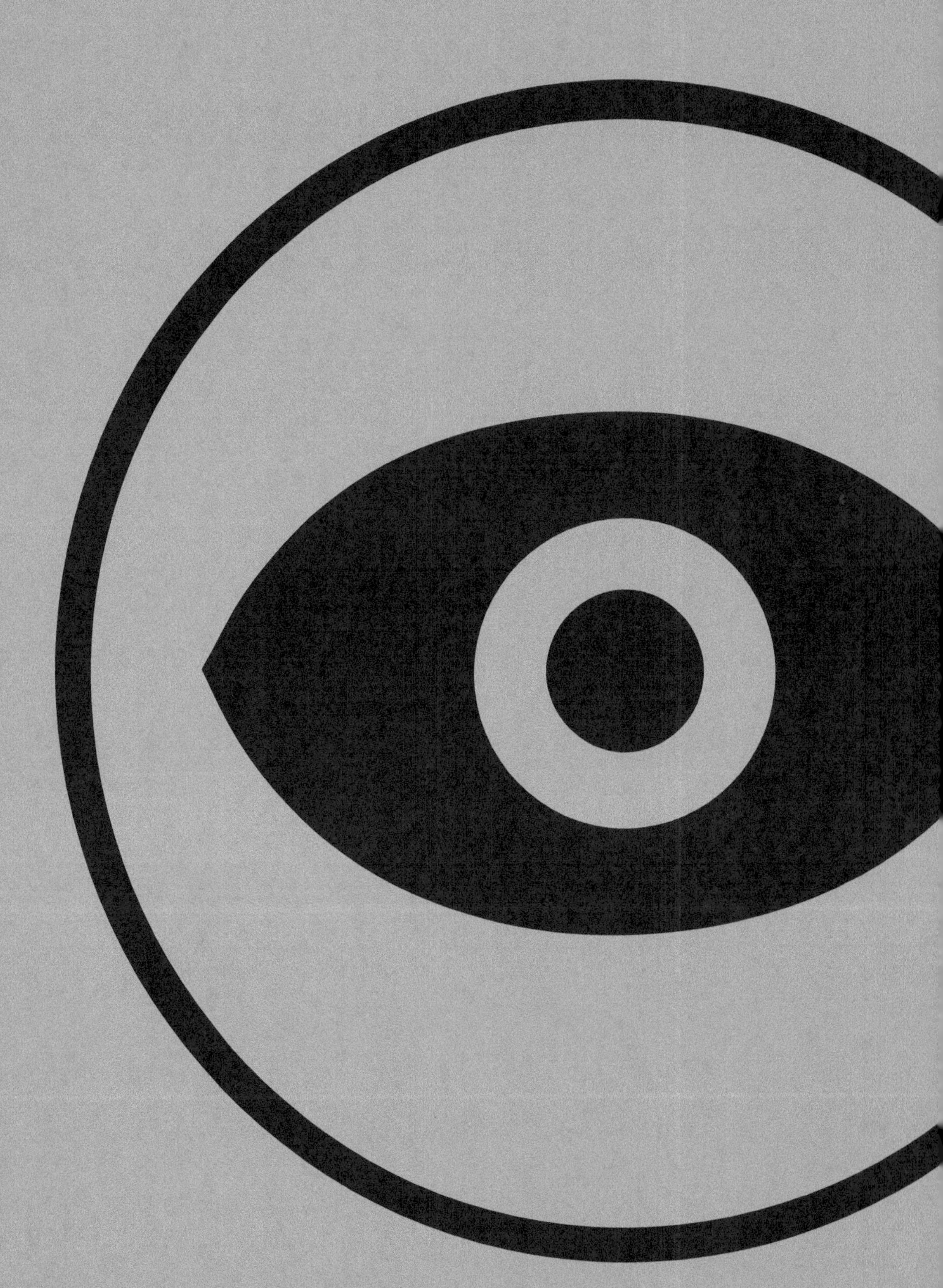

building should have a door, roof, windows, and walls. The Group tool will enable you to organize every layer and ensure that they all stay together whenever you are making the design.
Ungroup: You can likewise detach a design made up of many layers by using the Ungroup tool. It only does the opposite of what "Group" does.
Duplicate: This tool is self-explanatory. It duplicates whichever layer you choose on the Canvas.
Delete: This tool gets rid of the layers you choose. It will delete it permanently away from the Canvas.

Black canvas:
This layer is located on the Right panel. It enables you to modify the current Canvas color. If you are trying out different looks on your design, this option can place your design against numerous backgrounds.

Layer visibility:
This icon in the image above indicates the visibility of your design or layer. You will find it on all layers on the

Panel. It can be used when you're designing, and you observe that a particular element or segment looks odd; you can then click on the icon to get it hidden. Doing that will make sure you do not remove it permanently if you want it back later. Hidden items can be recognized with a visible cross mark.

Slice, weld, attach, flatten, and contour
It is vital to study how to utilize these five tools maximally. They will always come in handy, regardless of whatever you are designing.

Slice: Cricut made this tool for its users to carve out shapes, texts, and diverse elements from an entire design.

Weld: This is majorly used for merging shapes to form a new one. If you desire to make something different or creative with your design, you can combine different shapes.

Attach: Attach is more like an advanced version of the "Group" tool. It joins shapes and modifies their colors to fit the background color you are using. These changes will still be in effect even after you're done cutting.

Flatten: This tool will be handy when you're about printing different shapes. To flatten other forms, select the layers you desire to print, and then pick the "Flatten" option.

Contour: You can use this option if you de-

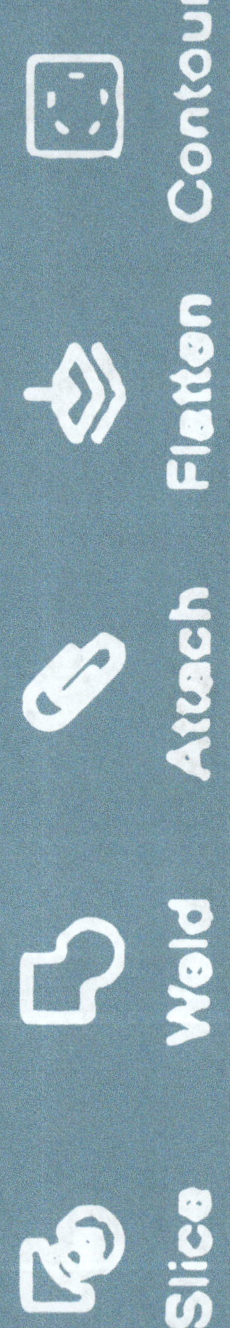

sire to hide an entire layer or a small part of a layer of design. However, this can only be done when the layers in your design can be separated.
Color sync

This tool is designed for balancing out your design and background colors. It can likewise be used to change diverse shades of a design color to a single color. As the name implies, Color Sync synchronizes the colors.
Left panel

The Left Panel consists of every option needed for inserting. Shapes, images, texts, and even ready-to-cut projects can be added. With the Left Panel, you can insert everything you want to cut. The Left Panel has seven options; let's quickly explore them all consecutively.
New

This option can be selected when you desire a new page. This new page is different from the page that you are designing with. It is better to save all your current designs before moving on to the page you just created. This is done to keep your plans in case you'll be needing them later. If you don't save before moving to the page you just created, your previous designs will be

lost.
Templates

A template allows you to preview how your design will look after cutting it out on a specific kind of fabric, such as a bag or a t-shirt. If you are making a bag with an iron-on design, it'll show you an image of your bag, and the design can now be placed on that template so that you can start planning the appearance of the bag in reality.

Templates will not cut out a real backpack for you, but they'll explain what the designs look like when they are cut out.
Projects

If you are ready to start cutting, then go to "Projects." You'll choose your project, make edits, modify it to suit your taste, and then click the "Make It" option. Several projects are available for users with Cricut Access membership, and some projects are accessible by purchase only. Apart from both means, only a few projects are free.
Images

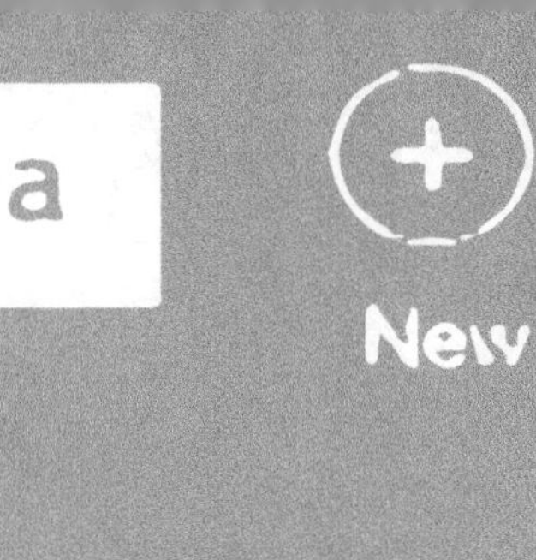

a

New

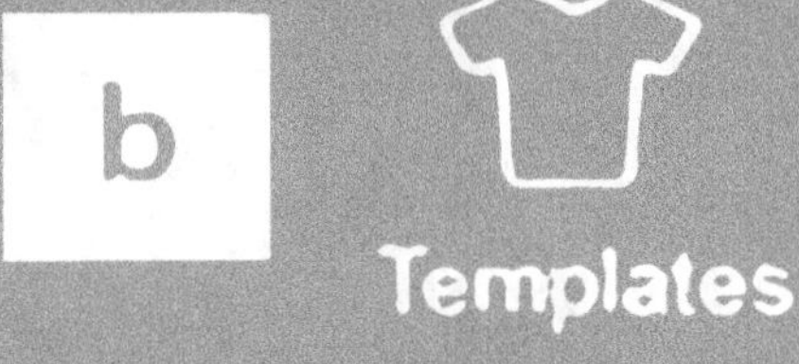

b

Templates

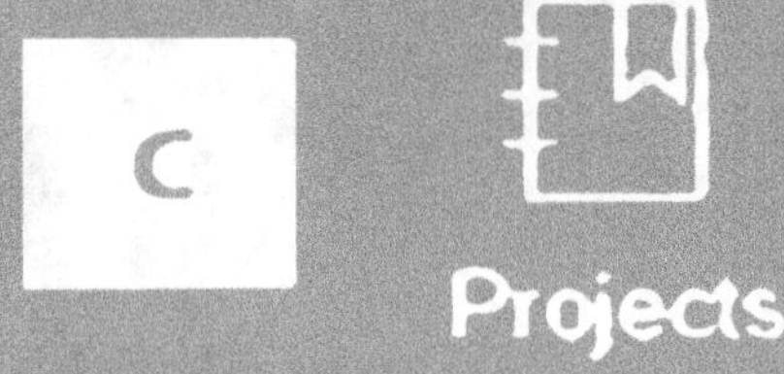

c

Projects

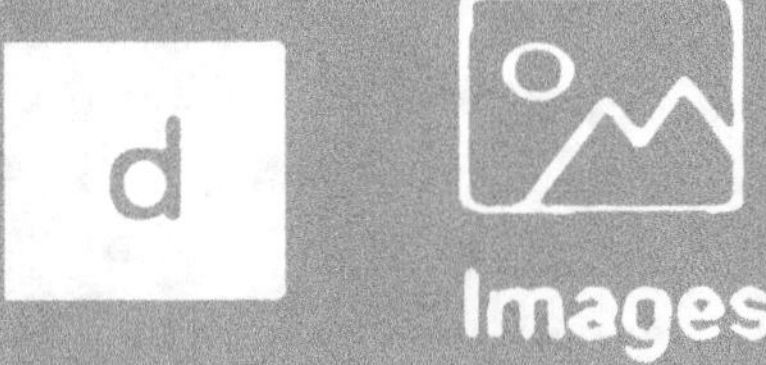

d

Images

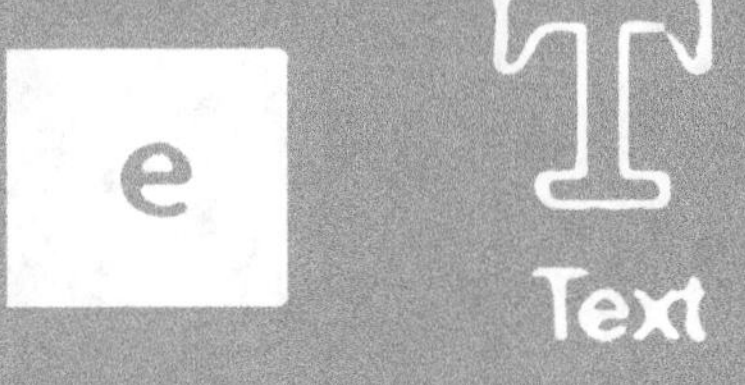

e

Text

f

Shapes

g

Upload

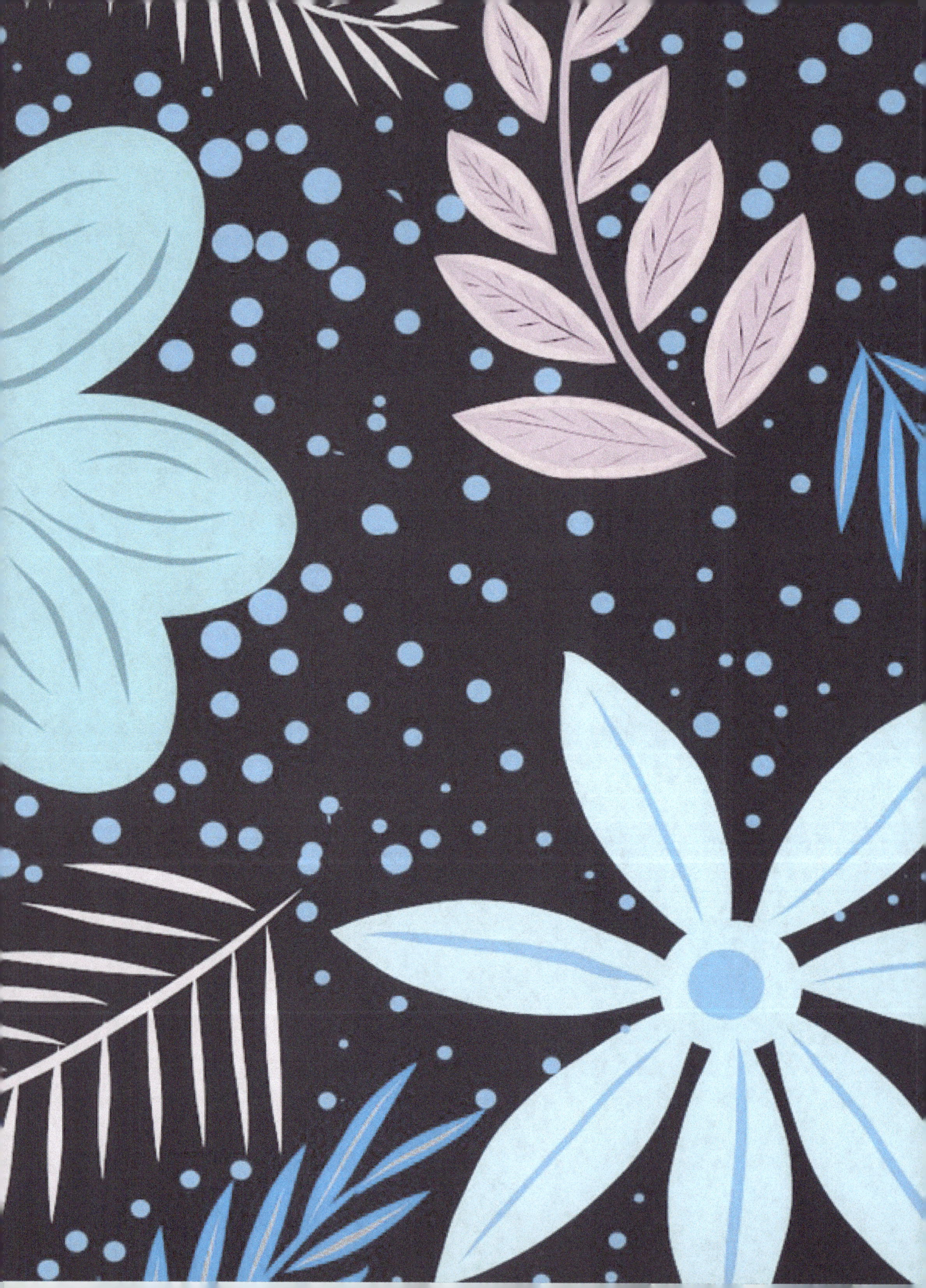

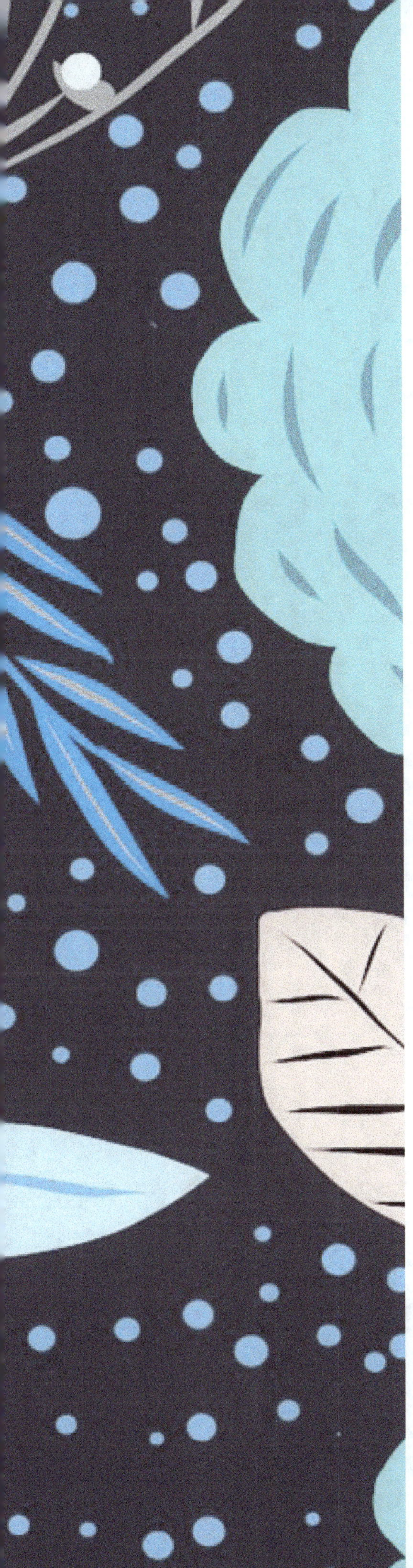

Images enable you to spice up your designs by adding a personal touch. With this tool, you can insert pictures that are provided on the Design Space for you. Cricut even offers free images each week, though some of them come with Cricut Access.

Text

The text tool enables you to include texts to your designs or only on the Canvas area. Clicking the "Text" tool opens a little window, indicating that you should add your text. You can add text and also customize the color and font.

Shapes

This tool is used when you wish to add a shape to your Canvas area. The Design Space provides some shapes for its users: square, triangle, hexagon, pentagon, heart, star, and octagon. There is likewise the "Score Line" tool located under the "Shapes" option. You can utilize this tool for folding these shapes to form other diverse shapes, particularly when you're making cards.

Upload

The "Upload" tool is the last tool you will find in the "Left Panel." This tool enables you to carry out file and image uploads, excluding the ones provided by Cricut. With this, images and patterns can be uploaded.

Elementary Functions

Functions and tools are almost the same things. You can know the parts of a device, and you can see the process of a process. However, what you regard as functions on the design space are used to make edits, organize, or tweak the Canvas area. Let us proceed and check out some of the available parts on the Cricut Design Space.
Top panel

The Top Panel is the only pane that is always full of activities. There are two different sub-panels under the Top Panel. Generally, the Top Panel is for organizing and making general editing on layers of design and elements.

First Subpanel

This enables a user to name their projects,

save them, and finally cut it. You can also find the options to save, name, and send your project for cutting on the Cricut machine in this subpanel.

Toggle menu: This option enables you to perform account and subscription management. This menu likewise allows you to update your Design Space, calibrate your Cricut machine, and perform some other operations.

Project name: Apparently, you can use this function to name your project. The project's default name will be "Untitled," it will always be like that until you rename it to something unique you can identify the project with.

My projects: This serves as a library for all your saved projects on the Design Space. So, this makes it possible to access old projects easily.

Save: This option gets your project saved into the Design Space library. It would help if you always kept your work to have issues when your browser crashes or stops responding.

Cricut maker / Cricut explore: When using the Design Space for the first time, a question will pop up to inquire if you're making use of a Cricut Explore machine from the Series or a Cricut Maker. Cricut Maker stands as the most advanced machine made by Cricut, and therefore, it provides several benefits on the Design Space more than other devices you will find in the Explore Series.

Make it: Click "Make It" after you have uploaded your files so that it can start cutting. The software categorizes your projects based on their colors, and if you are making plans to cut two or more projects, you can use this tool to increment the tasks you wish to cut.

Second Subpanel

The second subpanel is a menu for editing. It enables you to arrange, organize, and edit fonts and images on the canvas area.

Undo   redo:

Clicking "Undo" will revert a recent activity or action, and it is mostly used when a mistake is made or when an undesired move has been made. "Redo" does the opposite of "Undo," it brings back a deleted or reverted activity or action, and it is mostly used when something needed has been mistakenly deleted.

Cut under (line type)

You will find this line type on every layer present in the Canvas area. After

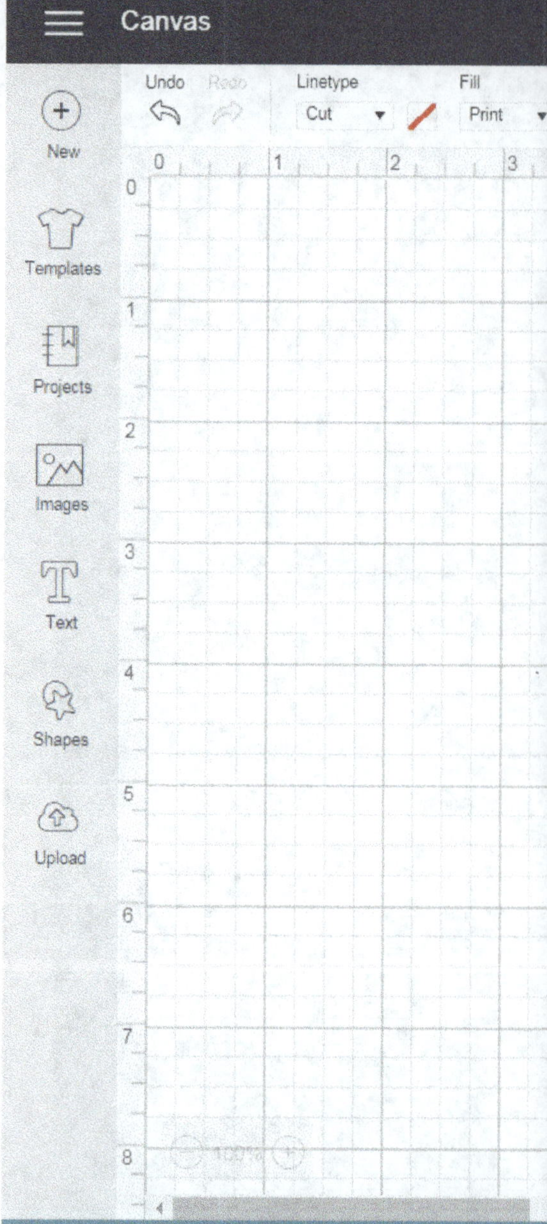

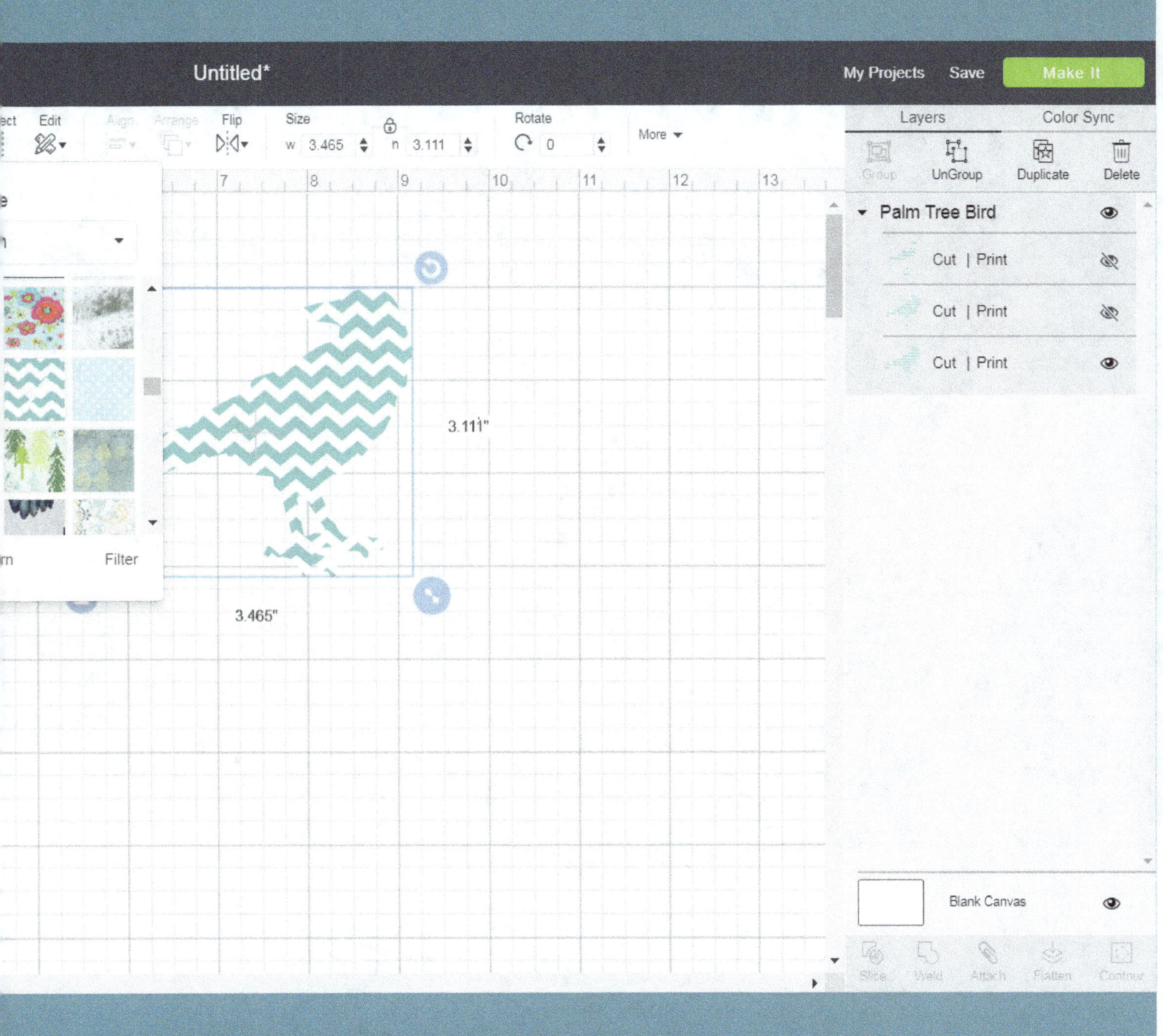

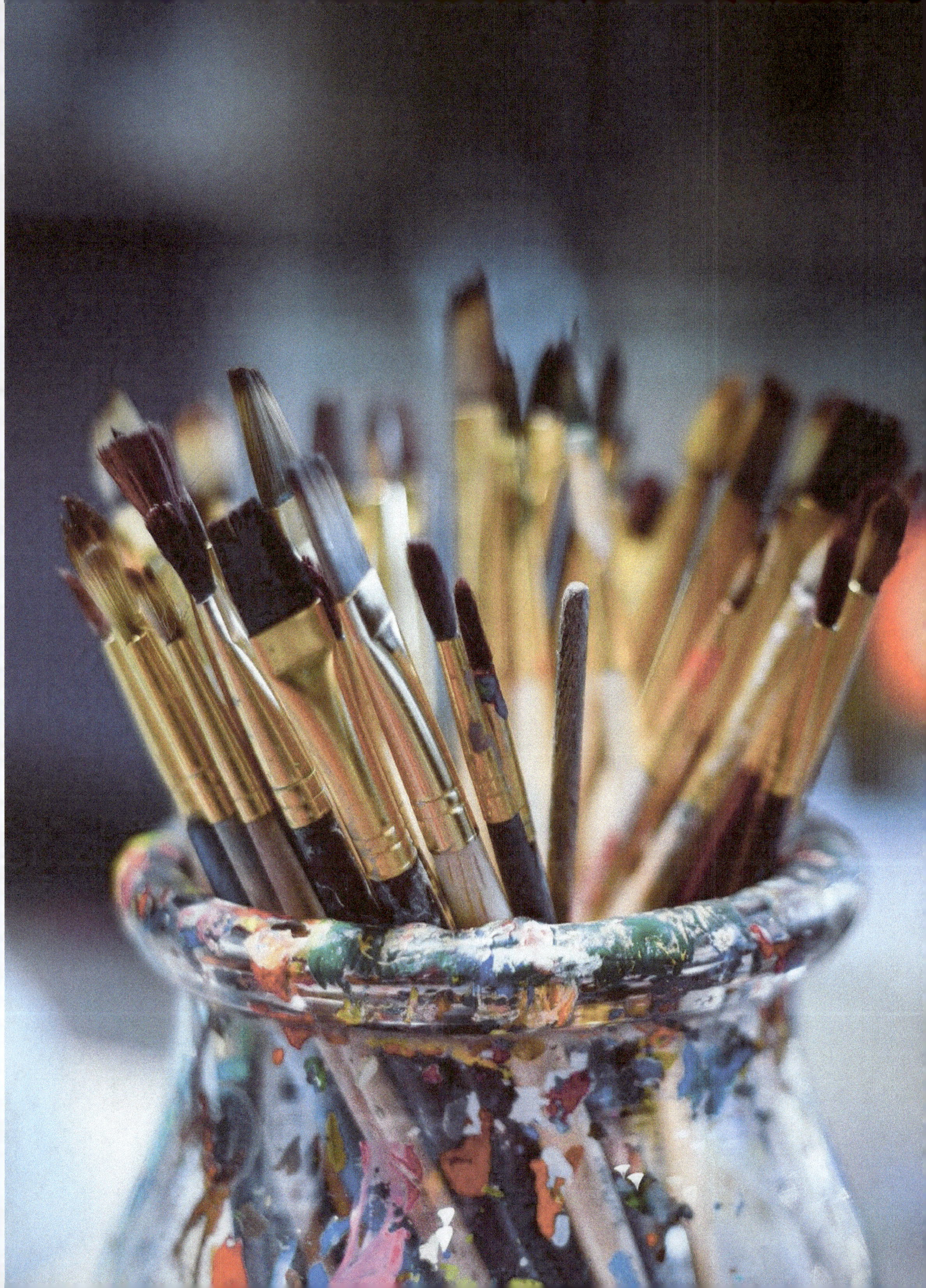

picking the "Make It" option, your Cricut machine starts cutting the designs that are on your Canvas area. This function enables you to alter the fill and colors of your layers.

Draw (line type):

Cricut likewise enables you to draw and write on the designs you create. When you choose this Line type, you are given several choices of various Cricut pens. You can utilize these pens to make drawings in the Canvas area. In this Line type, whenever you click "Make It," instead of cutting, your machine starts drawing or writing.

Score (line type): This function does almost the same thing as the "Scoring Line" tool in the Left Panel. It is just more advanced. Selecting this function for any of your layers will make it look like the coating has been scored. After that, click on "Make it" will get the materials achieved by your Cricut machine instead of having it cut.

A scoring wheel or scoring stylus will always be needed whenever you want to score. And only the latest machine, the Cricut Maker, can work with the scoring wheel.

Engrave, Wave, Deboss, and Perf (Line type): These tools were recently released by Cricut. Therefore, only Cricut Maker users can make use of them. Additionally, it must have the newest version of the Design Space app before these new tools can be accessed. These tools enable you to make significant effects on many materials.

Fill Cricut majorly designed this function to print and make patterns. However, you can only use this function "Cut" has been selected as a Line type.

Print:

Every Cricut user loves this function. Even though you can't do without it if you want your design to be cuttable, you'll also find this function a little bit interesting.

It enables you first to have your design printed out and then cut them out. If you want to print out your plan, click on "Make It" when the "Fill" option is active. After that, send the files to your home printer before you start sending them to the Cricut machine for cutting.

Edit

This function consists of three options on the menu list. You'll find a "Cut" option, which enables you to copy. Clear elemen-

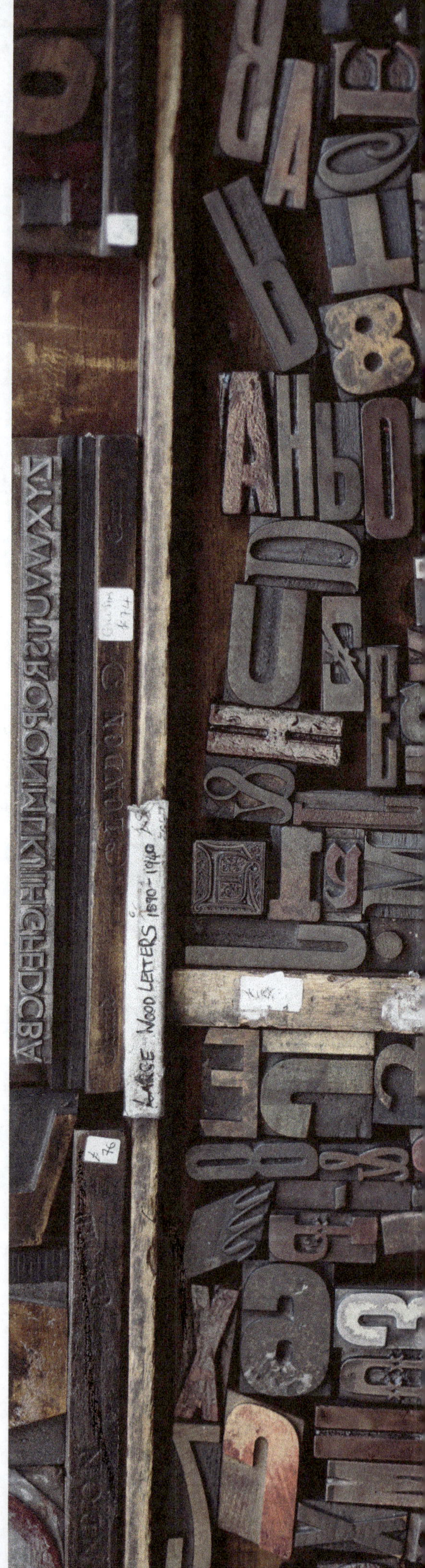

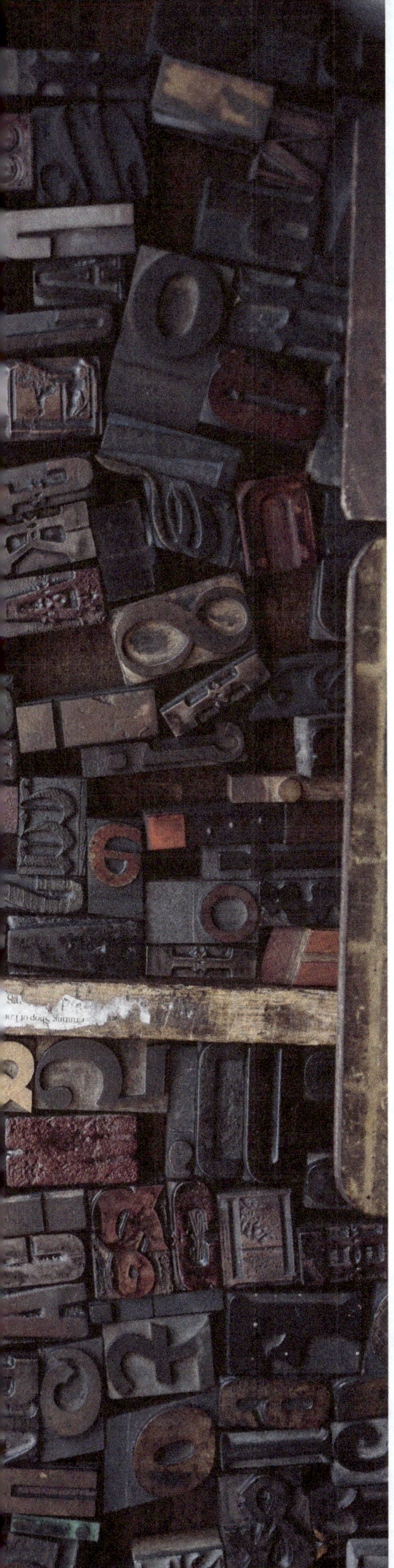

ts from the Canvas, you'll find the "Copy" option, which allows you to copy the same component without getting it cleared, and lastly, you'll find the "Paste" option, which helps you insert the element you have copied or cut.

Select All: Clicking this will highlight everything you have on your Canvas area.

Align: There're several diverse options under this function, and it's essential for you to master all these options. Let's take a look at them;

Align Left: This function makes sure that every element is left-aligned. However, the movement will solely depend on the item at the end of the left side.

Center Horizontally: This will horizontally align every design element.

Align Right: This function makes sure that every element is right-aligned. However, the movement will solely depend on the item at the end of the right side.

Align Top: This will automatically align all the selected elements to the Canvas page's uppermost part.

Center Vertically: This will vertically align every design element.

Align Bottom: This functions as the exact opposite of the "Align Top" function. It aligns elements or layers to the bottom.

Center: Clicking this function will center-align all elements that are either vertically aligned or horizontally aligned.

Distribute: This enables you to distribute the spacing between layers or elements equally. We have two types;

Distribute Horizontally

Distribute Vertically

Flip

This function will allow you to see the reflection of your designs. You can see this function as a mirror-view of your designs. There are two options available for this function:

Flip Horizontal

Flip Vertical

Arrange

The "Arrange" function enables you to arrange elements such as designs, texts, or images to the back or front of others. There are four types of arrangement, and they are as follows:

Send to Back: This moves the design or element you select to the farthest back of other elements or designs.

Move Backward: What makes this function and the "Send to Back" function different

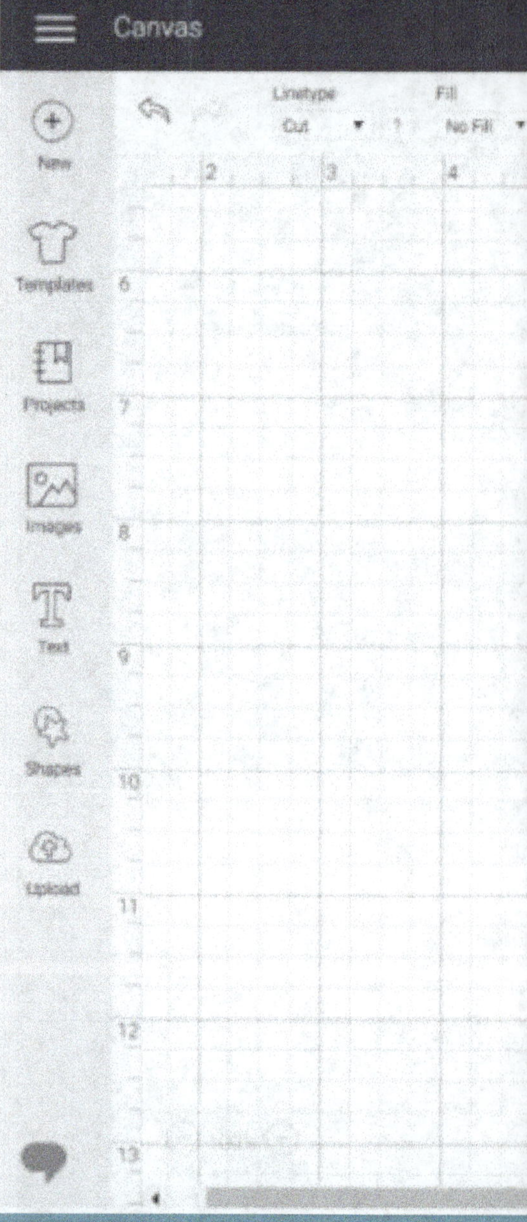

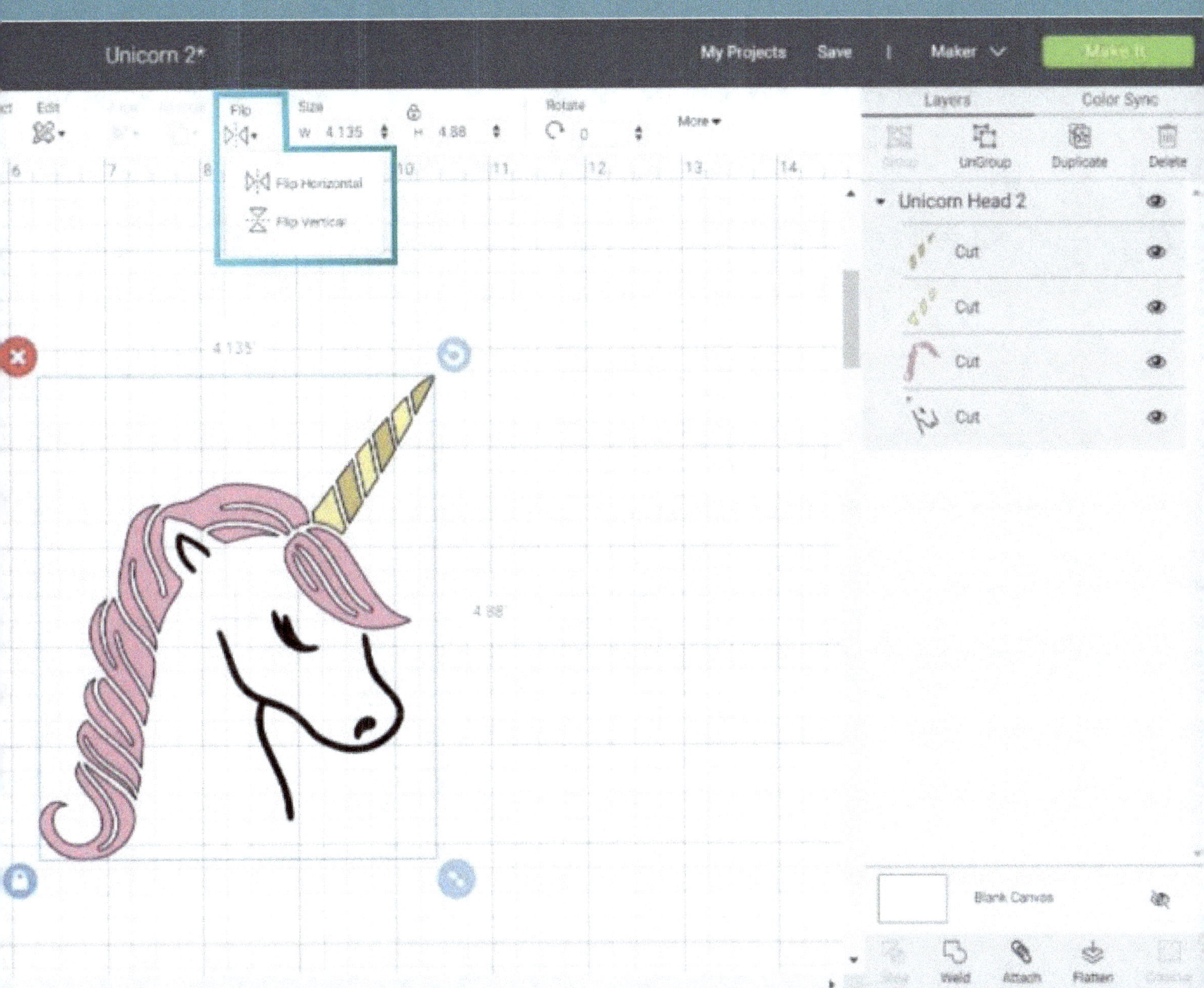
Unicorn 2*
My Projects   Save | Maker ⌄   Make It
Edit   Flip   Size   Rotate   More ▾
W 4.135   H 4.88   0
Flip Horizontal
Flip Vertical
Layers   Color Sync
Group   UnGroup   Duplicate   Delete
▾ Unicorn Head 2
Cut
Cut
Cut
Cut
Blank Canvas
Slice   Weld   Attach   Flatten   Contour

is that it moves an element or design back once. This allows you to control how further back you want a feature or design. Move Forward: This does the exact opposite of "Move Backward," you can control how further you want an element or design. Send to Front: This moves the design or element you select to the furthest front of other aspects or designs.
Size

This function enables you to alter an element's size or the whole design's size. Whatever you create within the Canvas Area has a specified scale, and you can use this to either decrease or increase the size. This is more useful when following a particular format for all the elements or the entire design.
Rotate

With this Design Space function, you can rotate elements or layers to your desired angle.
Position

  Since the Canvas area has gridlines, just like coordinates, you can use this function to find and pick a particular position for the element on the X and Y-axis.

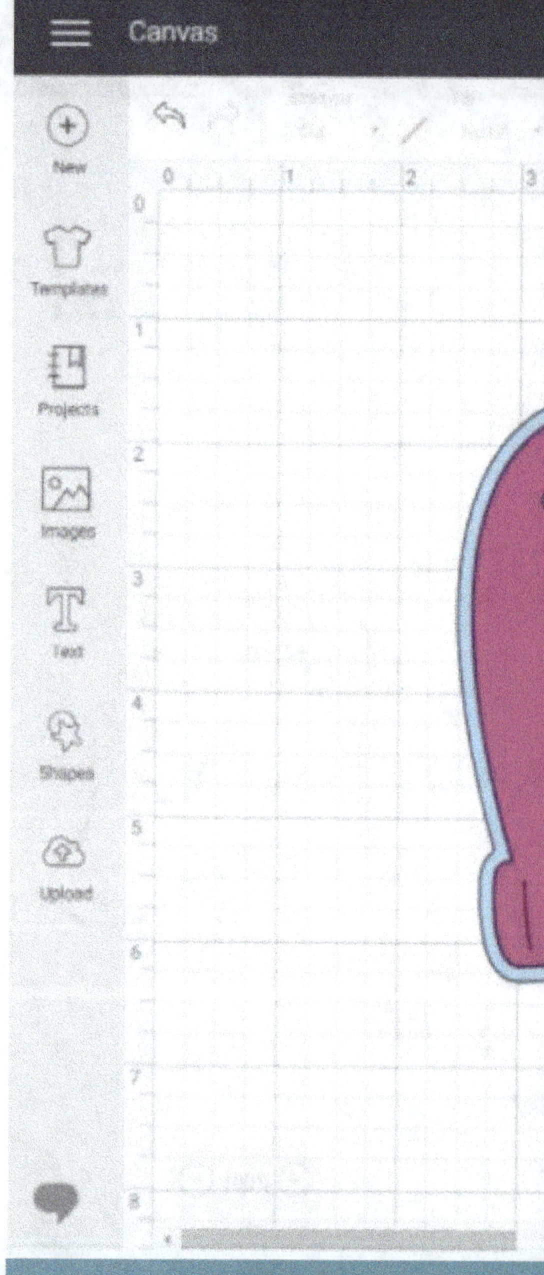

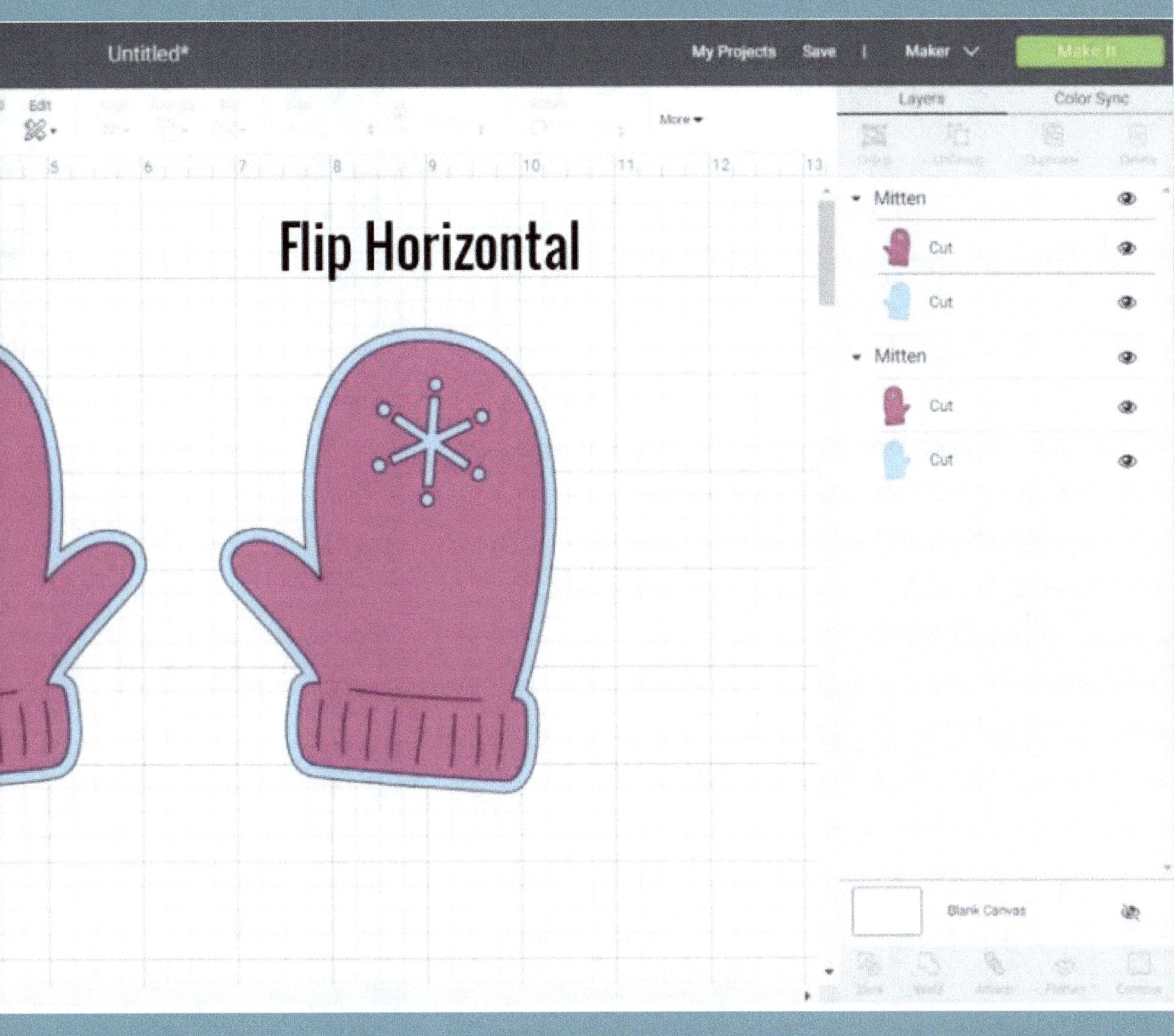
Untitled*
My Projects   Save | Maker ⌄   Make It
Edit
More ▾
Layers   Color Sync
Flip Horizontal
Mitten
Cut
Cut
Mitten
Cut
Cut
Blank Canvas

Font

There are various types of fonts on Cricut for all users with Cricut Access membership. You can use your default font or purchase different fonts from Cricut if you do not have a Cricut Access subscription.
Font Size

This enables you to either decrease or increases your font size.
Line Space

This is particularly suitable for use whenever you wish to make sure that all texts on your designs are orderly or manually spaced.
Letter Space

This function enables you to decide how much space you want between letters.
Style

This consists of "Regular," which is already applied by default, "Bold," which makes the font thick, "Italic," which tilts the font sideways, and then "Bold Italic," which combines both the Bold and Italic function.
Curve

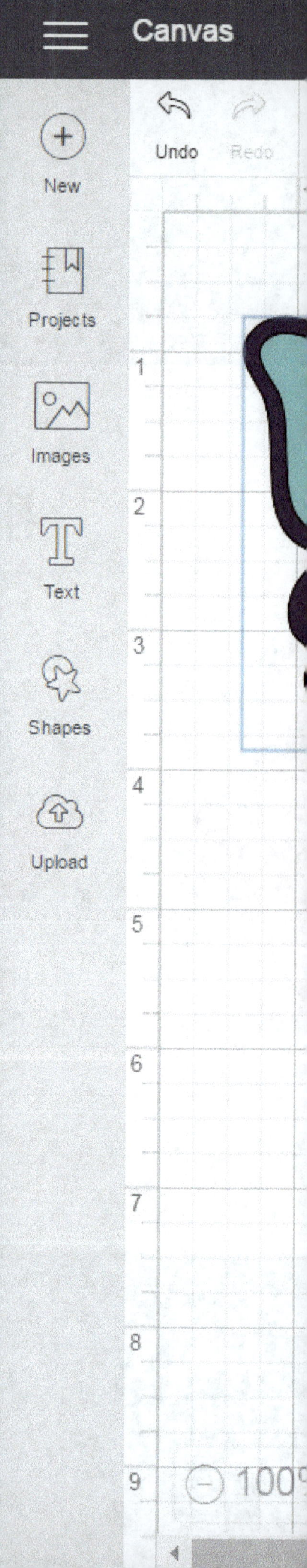

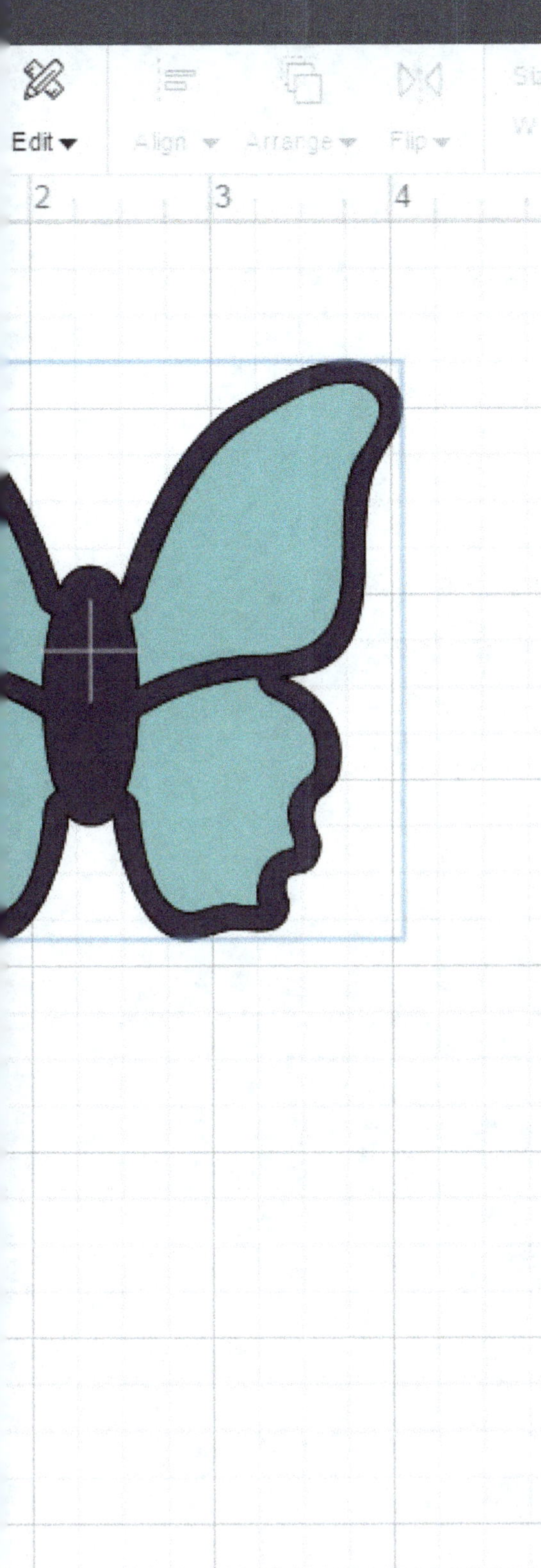

You can also design your texts by using the curve setting. You can curve your text upwards or inwards. You can even curve your readers into a circle.
Advanced

You'll find this function on the top editing panel, and it's the last function on the board.
Ungroup to letters: This enables you to detach all letters into single layers apiece.
Ungroup to lines: This enables you to break paragraphs on different lines.
Ungroup to layers: This option is available only on Cricut Access. It can also be purchased. It is quite tricky, though; you have to be fully conscious of what you're doing.

Canvas area

This stands as the significant workspace of the Design Space. You can find all the designs and elements that you are working on on this platform.

Canvas grid and dimensions

Gridlines are the lines that cover your Canvas Area on the Design Space and divide the area into small squares. The Canvas area resembles the cutting mat, which gives you the feeling of designing your actual cutting mat on the screen. You can use centimeters or inches, and you can also decide to turn the grid off in your settings.

Zoom out or in

You can use this function to expand or reduce the focus of a design or an element on your canvas area. This function can be utilized if you desire to make your arrangement bigger or smaller to work on it comfortably or if you just want to focus on a design or an element.

Selection

Whenever you select two or more layers, the color of the selection turns blue, and the four corners surrounding it enable you to adjust the layer. You'll see an "X" in red color; click on it when you wish to delete those layers.

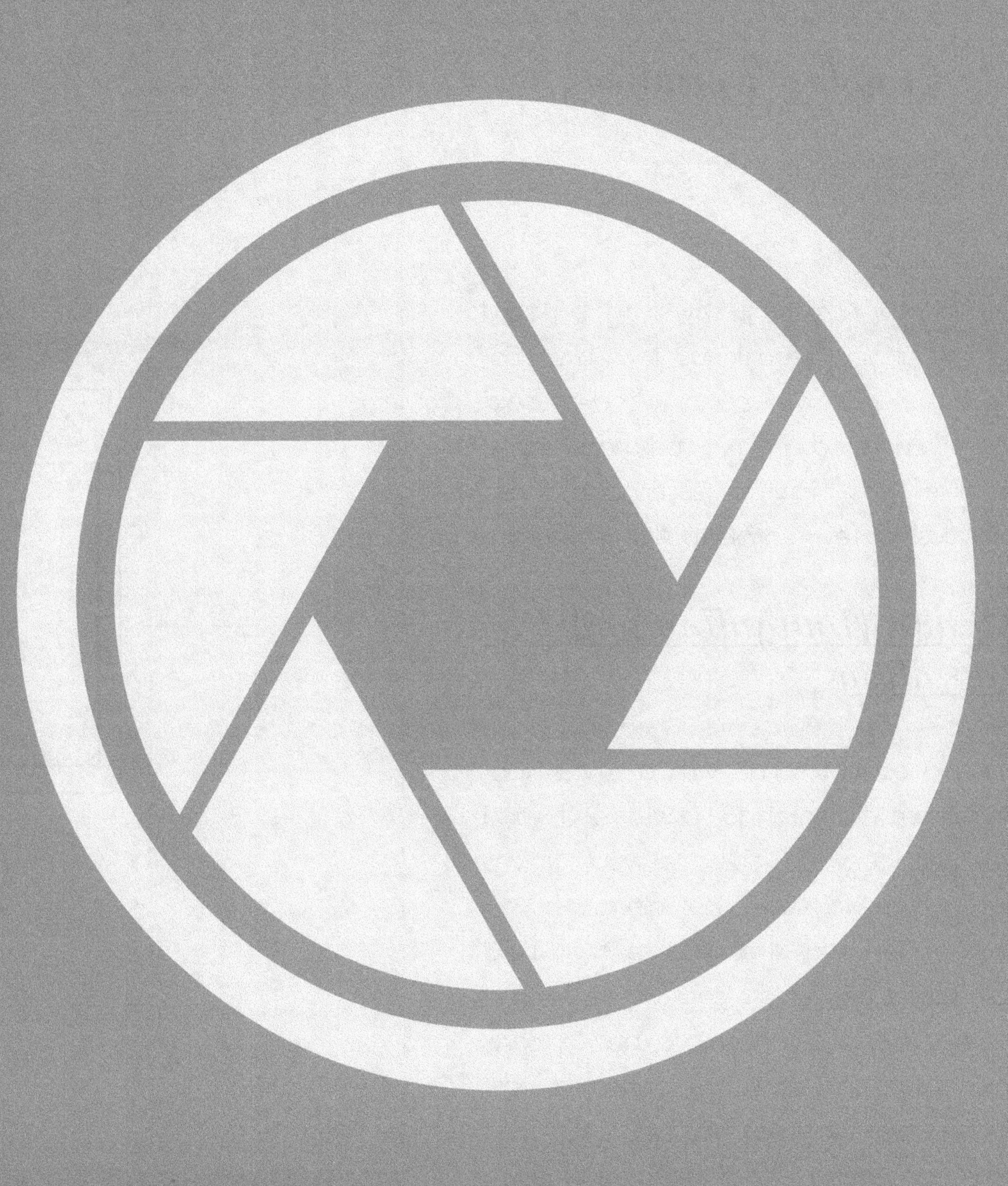

Chapter 4
Complex Operations

Cricut machines are pretty straightforward with what you need to do to make simple designs, but you might wonder about some more complex operations. Here, we'll tell you how to accomplish these with just a few simple button presses.

Blade Navigation and Calibration

The blades that come with a Cricut machine are essential to understand, and you will need to calibrate your knives every time you use your device.

Each blade needs this because it will help you figure out which level of depth and pressure your cut needs to be. Typically, each blade needs to be calibrated only once, which is great because you don't have to spend time doing this each time. Once you've done it once, it will

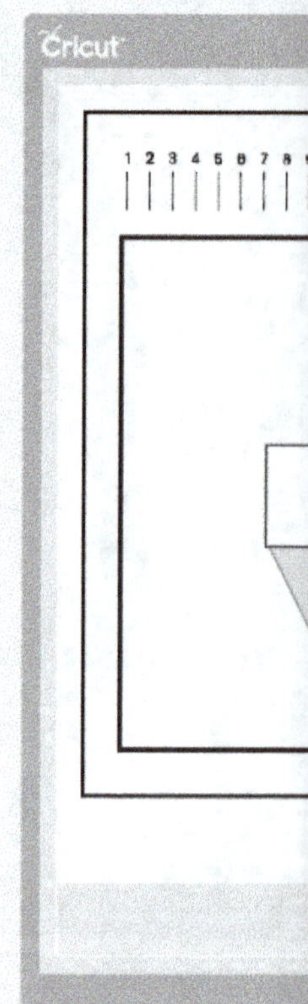

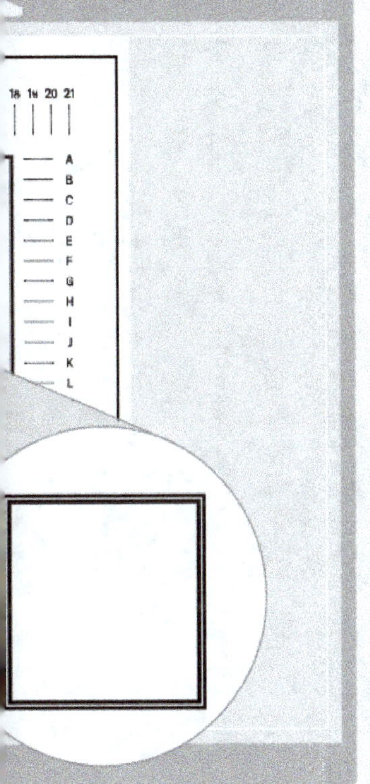

Test Cut

Cricut machine scanning for calibration sheet on mat

Continue →

stay calibrated, but if you decide to change the blades' housings or use them in another machine, you'll need to calibrate it again.

So, if you plan on using a knife blade and then a rotary cutter, you'll want to make sure that you do recalibrate - and make sure you do this before you start with your project. It is straightforward to do this, though, which is why it's encouraged.

To calibrate a blade, you launch the Design Space, and from there, you open the menu and choose calibration. Then, select the edge that you're going to put in. For this explanation, let's say you're using a knife blade.

Put that blade in the clamp B area, do a test cut, copy paper into the mat, and then load it into the machine.

Press continue, then press the go button on the machine. It will then do everything you need for the item itself, and it will start to cut.

You can then choose which calibration is best for your blade, but the first one is usually good enough.

Set Paper Size

Setting paper size in a Cricut machine is pretty simple. You will want to use this with either cartridge or Design Space for what you'd like to make. This also comes with a cutting mat, and you'll want to load this up with paper so that you can use it.

To do this, you'll want to make sure that you have it plugged in, then go to the project preview screen. Suppose you choose a more oversized material than the mat size. In that case, it will automatically be changed, and it'll be adjusted as necessary based on the size of the material you select.

You can choose the color, the size of the material, whether or not it'll mirror - and you can also choose to entirely skip the mat, too, if you don't want that image printed just yet.

Note that the material size menu does offer sizes that are bigger than the largest mat available.

If you're planning on using the print then cut mode, understand that it's limited to a print area of 8.5x11 inches, but again, you can choose these settings for yourself.

Load Last

To load that paper and image last is pretty simple. Remember the preview we discussed in the previous section? Remember that "skip this mat" step? Press that, and then go. You'll be able to skip this quite easily. It's one of

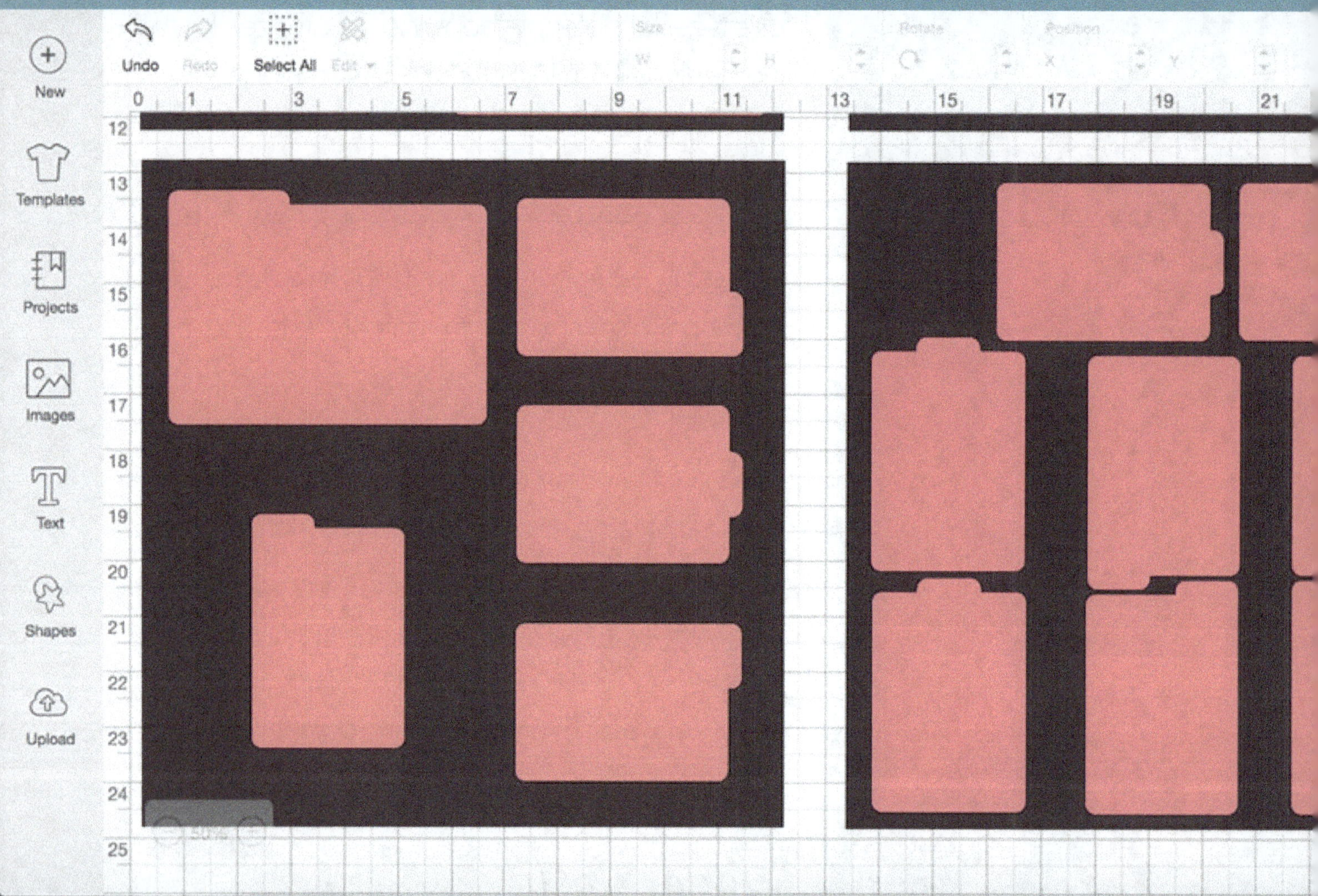

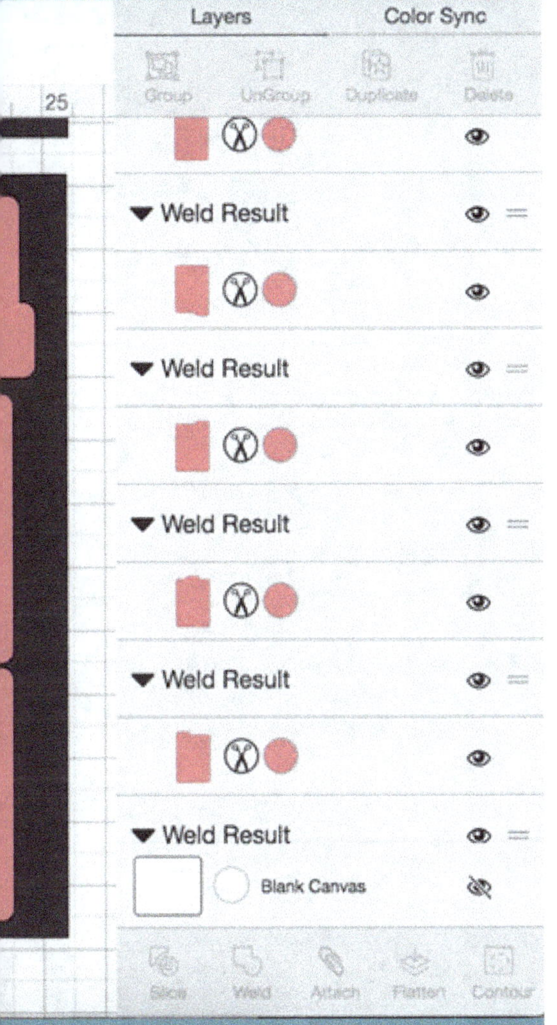

those operations that's a little different from what you may be used to, but if you want to skip design and don't want to work with it just yet, this is probably the best option for you to use. If you're worried about forgetting it, don't worry - Cricut will remind you.

Paper Saver

Saving paper is something you'll want to consider doing with a Cricut machine because it loves to eat up the form before you even start decorating. The Explore Air 2 appreciate it if you save paper, and there are a few ways to do so.

The first one is, of course, to halve your mats. But you don't need to do only that.

You can also go to the material saver option on the machine, which will automatically adjust and align your paper as best it can. Unfortunately, it's actually not directly stated on newer devices, but there is a way to save the report.

You'll want to create tabbed dividers to organize your projects and save them directly there.

The first step is to create a background shape. Make sure that the paper looks like a background. Go to conditions, and then select the square to make the square shape.

Next, once you've created squares to re-present paper, arrange this to move to the back so that the shapes are organized to save the most space on each mat. Then collect the items on top of where the background is and arrange them to fit on a singular mat.

Rotating is your best friend - you can use this feature whenever you choose objects, so you suggest getting familiarized with it.

Next, you hide the background at this point, and you do this by choosing the square and in Design Space, literally hiding this on the right side. Look at the eyeball on the screen, and you'll see a line through the eyeball. That means it's hidden.

Check over everything and fine-tune it at this point. Make sure they're grouped around one object, and make sure everything has measurements. Move these around if they're outside of the sizes required.

Once they're confirmed, you attach these on the right-hand side of Design Space, which keeps everything neatly together - they're all cut from the same sheet.

From here, repeat this until everything is neatly attached. It will save your paper, but will it save you time? That's debatable, of course.

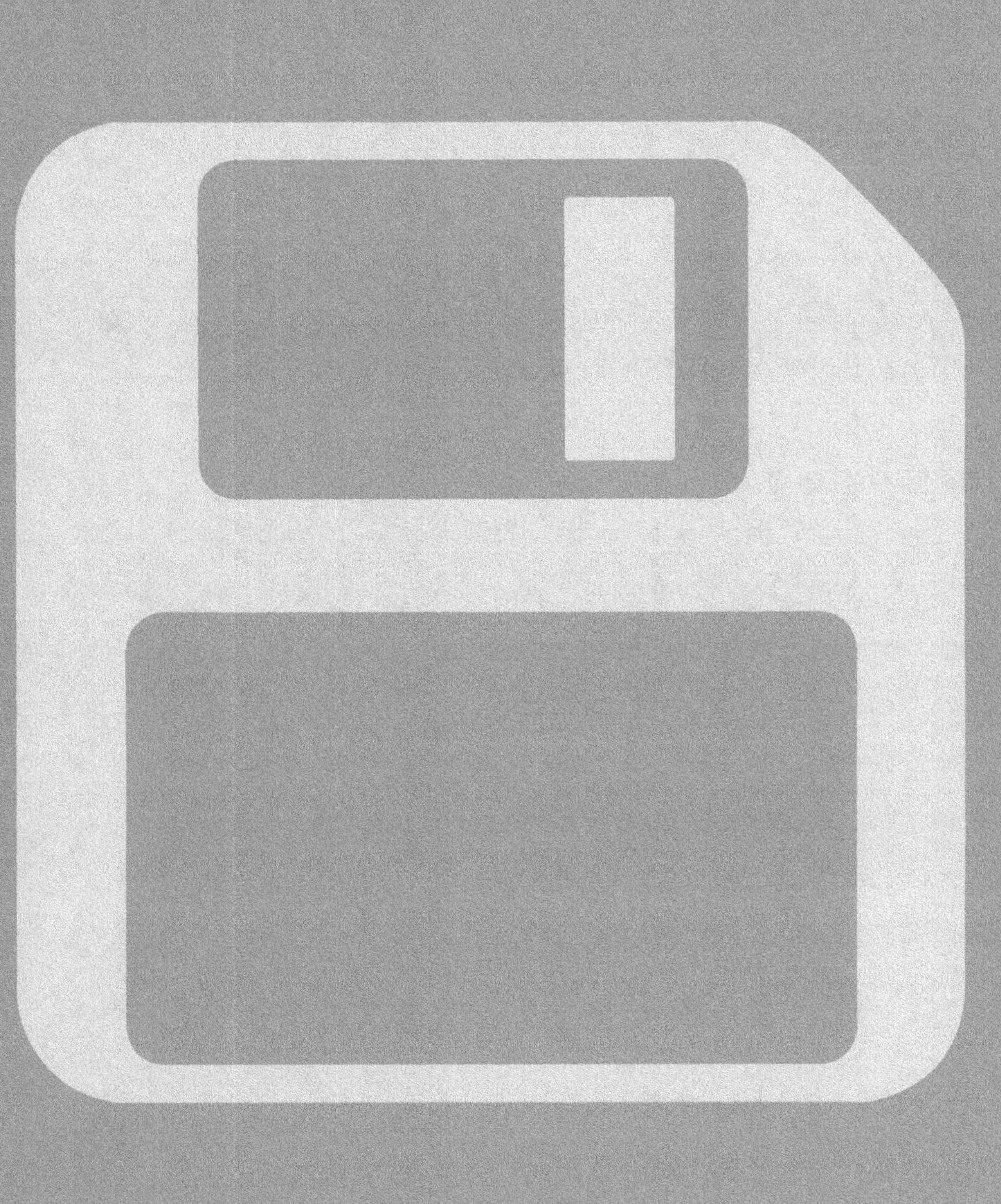

Speed Dial

So, the speed dial typically comes into play when you're setting the pressure and speed. Fast mode is one of the options available on the Explore Air 2 and the Maker machines, making the engine run considerably quicker than other models. You can use this with vinyl, cardstock, and iron-on materials. To set this, go to the cut screen. You'll have a lot of speed dials here and different settings. If you have the right material in place when choosing it, you'll be given the option to do it quickly with fast mode. From there, you simply tap or click on that switch to toggle this to the position for on. That will activate fast mode for that item.

It will make everything about two times faster, which means that if you're creating intricate swirl designs, it will take 30 seconds instead of the 73-second average it usually takes.

However, one downside to this is that it will sometimes make the cuts less precise because it's so fast that you'll want to move back to the regular mode for more delicate work.

This is all usually set with the smart-set dial, which will offer the right settings for you

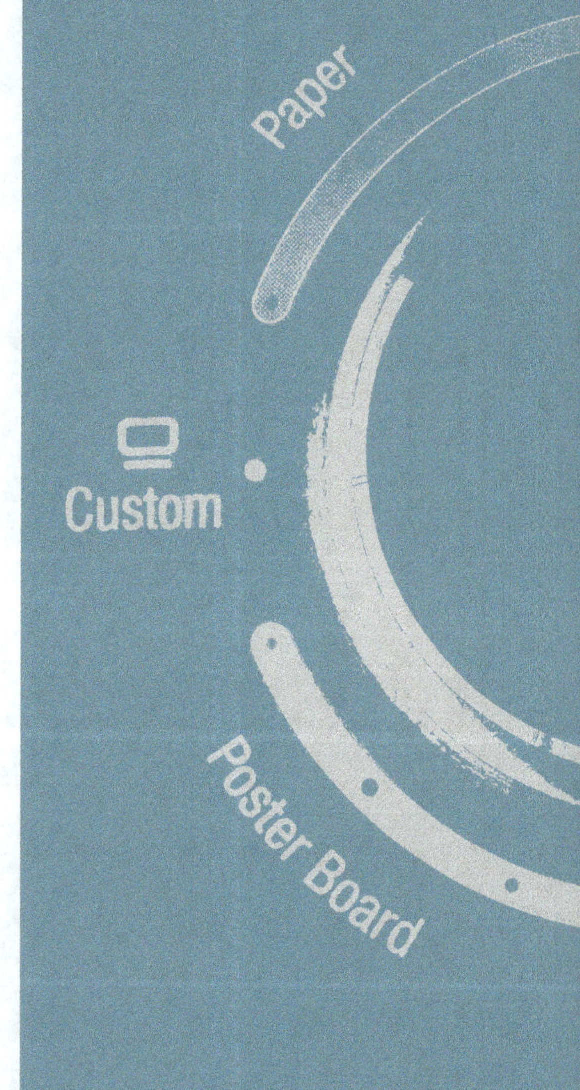

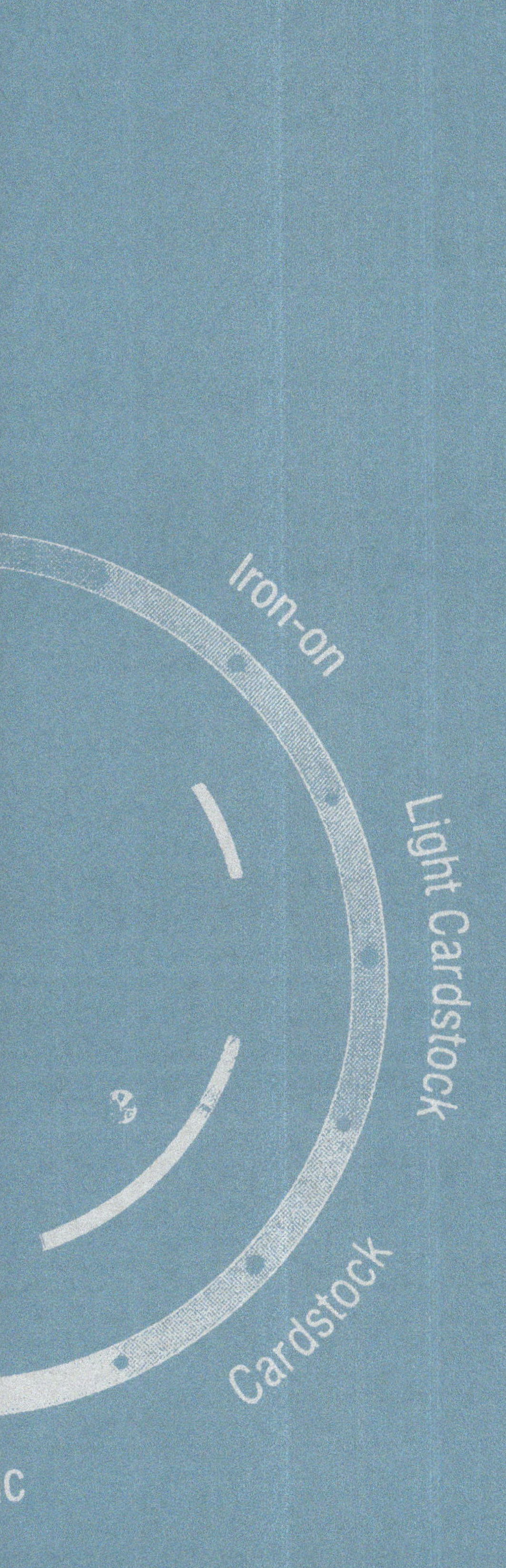

to get the best cuts that you can on any material you're using. Virtually, this dial eliminates you having to check the pressure on this manually.

To change the speed and pressure for a particular material that isn't already determined with the preset settings, you will need to select custom mode and choose what you want to create. Of course, the smart-set dial is better for the Cricut products and mats. If you notice that the blade is cutting too deep or not profound enough, there is a half-setting option on each material you can adjust to achieve the ideal cut.

Usually, the way you do this with the pre-set settings is to upload and create a project; the press goes, loads the mat, and then moves the smart-set dial on the machine itself to any environment. Let's select custom and choose the speed for this one. In Design Space, you choose the material, add the custom speed, and adjust these settings. You can even adjust the number of times you want the cut to be changed with the smart-set dial, too. Rate is something you can adapt to suit the material, which can help you struggle with putting together some right settings for your items.

Pressure Dial

Now, let's talk about pressure. Each piece of material will require different pressure settings. If you're not using enough pressure, the blade won't cut into the material, and if you use too much pressure, you'll end up missing the mat, which isn't what you want to do.

The smart-set dial kind of takes the guesswork out of it. You simply choose the setting that best fits your material, and from there, you let it cut. If you notice you're not getting a deep enough cut, you'll want to adjust it about half a setting to a better result. From there, adjust as needed.

But did you know that you can change the pressure on the smart-set dial for custom materials? Let's say you're cutting something very different, such as foil, and you want to set the pressure to be incredibly light so that the foil doesn't get shredded. What you do is load the material in, and you choose the custom setting. You can then select the material you plan to cut, such as foil - and if it's not on the list, you can add it.

From here, you're given pressure options. People will often go too heavy with their custom settings, so you suggest that you go

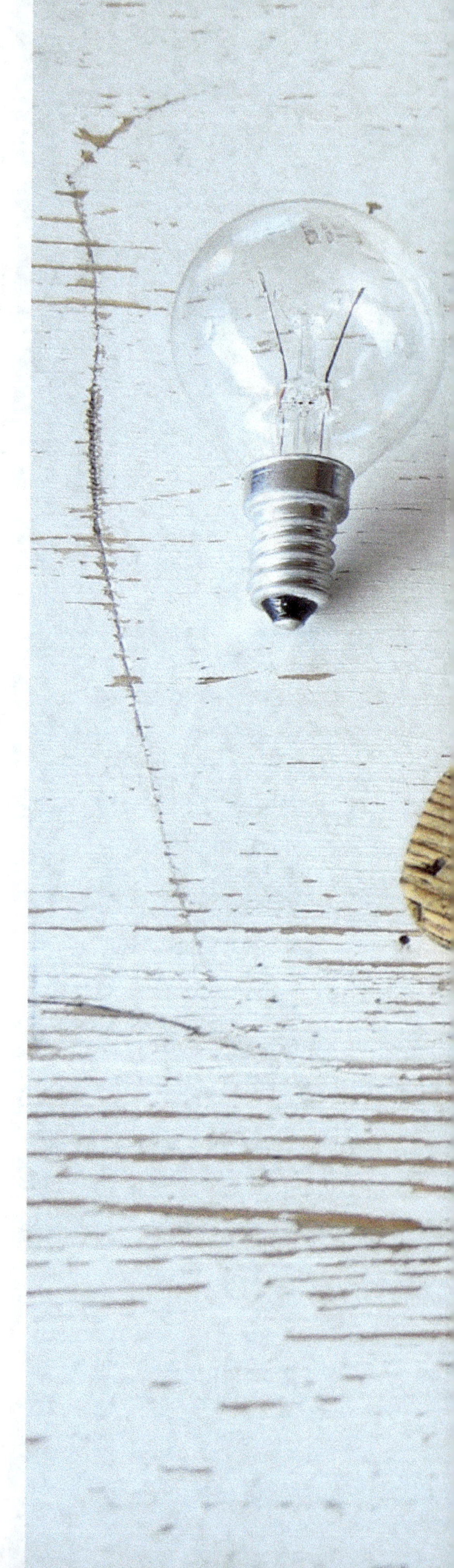

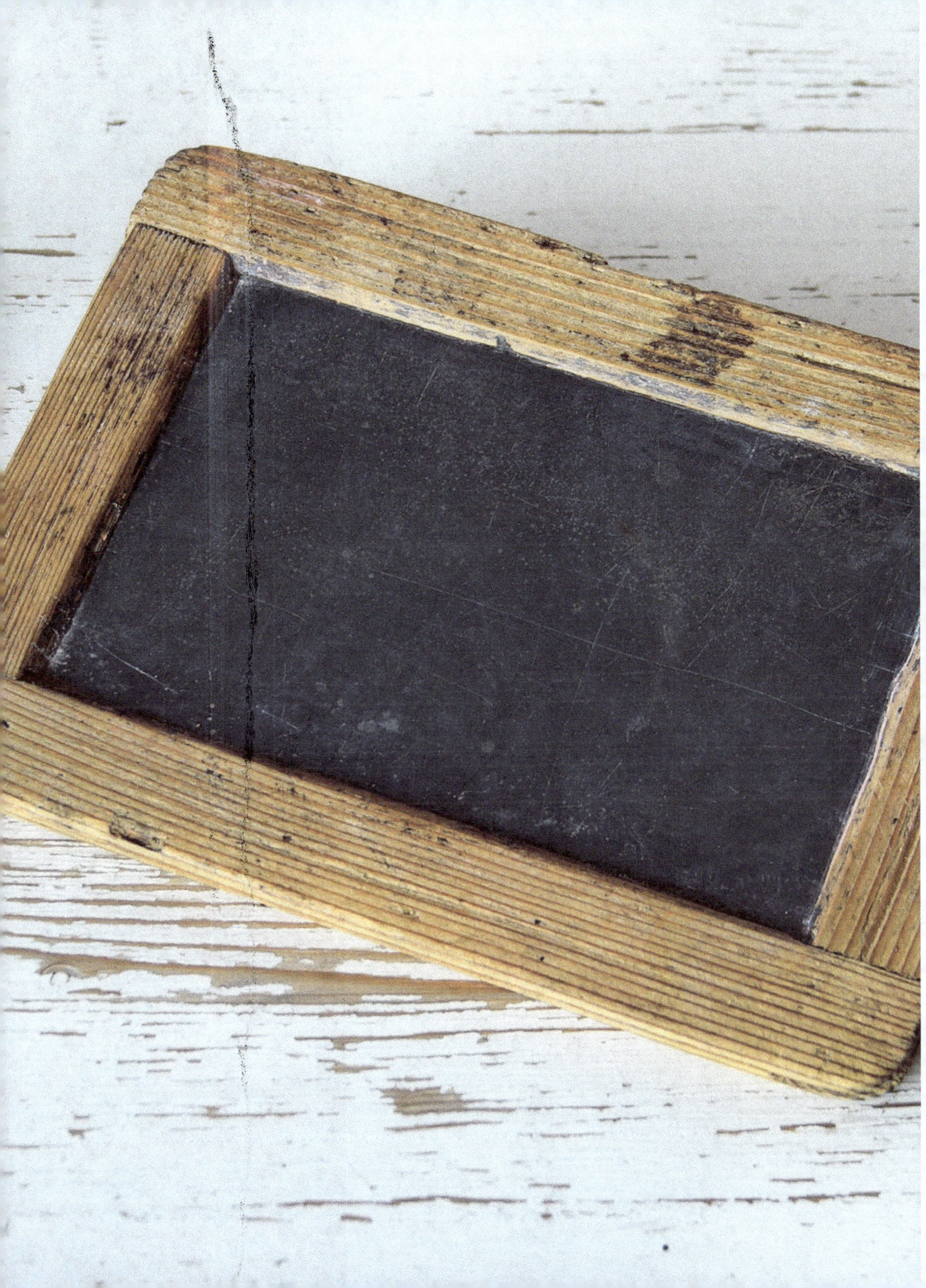

lighter for the first time and change it as needed. Several draggers go from low to high. If you need lots of pressure, obviously let it go higher. If you don't need much pressure, make sure it's left lower. You will also want to adjust the number of times the cut is done on a multi-cut feature item. This is a way for you to achieve multiple cuts for the item. They can be accommodating for those trying to get the right cut, or if the material is tough to cut, you don't suggest using this for very flimsy and thin material because it'll just waste your blade and the mat itself.

That's all there is to it! This is a great way to improve on your Cricut designs. You just press the change settings button to adjust your pressure, speed, or how many cuts you want, and then choose to save when you're done.

What if you don't like a setting, period? You can delete it, of course!

To delete, go to materials settings, and you'll see a little trash can next to it. Press the trash can, and the setting will be removed. Adjusting the pressure and cuts is part of why people love using Design Space, and it's a great feature to try.

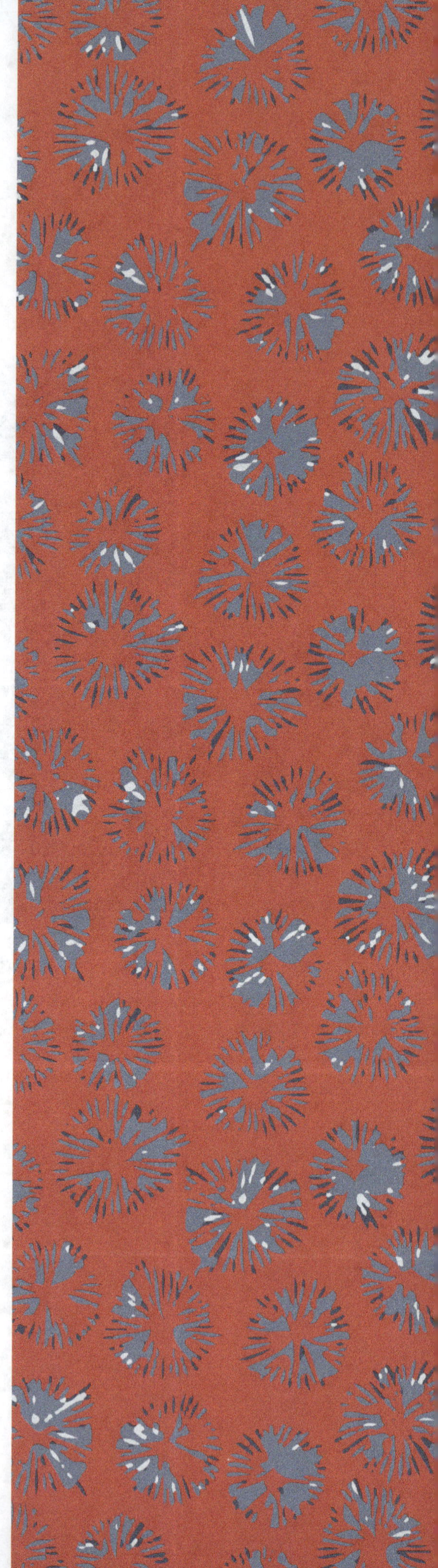

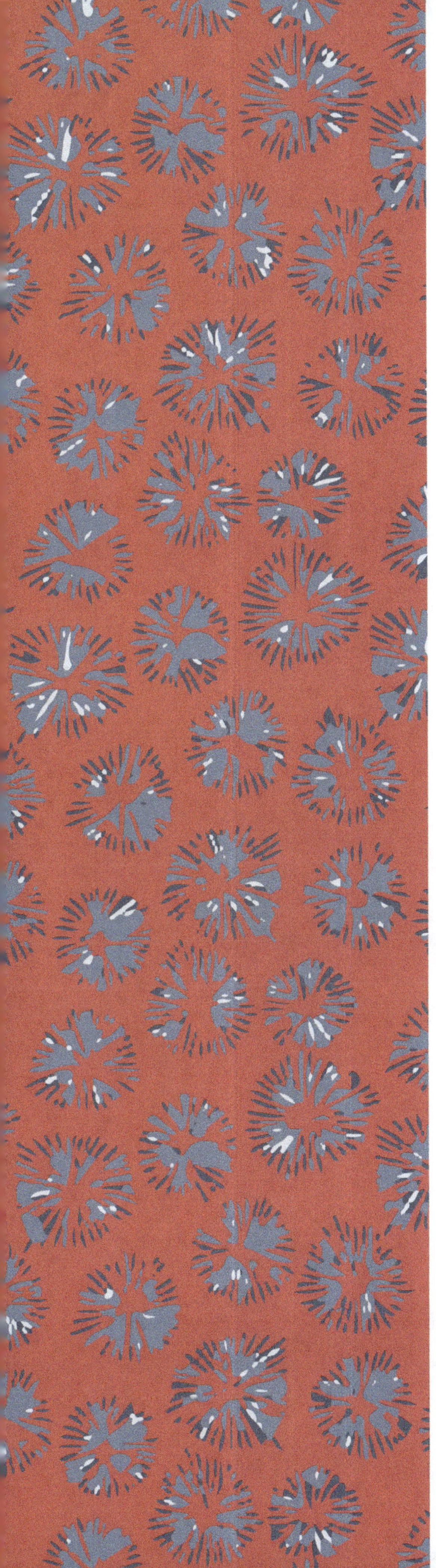

Cricut Design Space

Design Space lets you do many things with your Cricut machine. Here are a few things you can do with this convenient app:

You are attaching items to hold images in place and lets you use score lines.

We are arranging these to make them sit on the canvas in different layers.

Canvas, a tool that lets you arrange prints and vectors to use the various devices with them.

Contouring, which is a tool that lets you hide image layers quickly so they're not cut out.

Color sync, which lets you use multiple colors in one project to reduce the material differences.

Cut buttons, which will start cuts.

Make it button: this is the screen that lets you see the designs being cut.

Draw lines: lets you draw with the pen to write images and such.

Fill: lets you fill in a pattern or color on an item.

Flipping items, flip it horizontally or vertically by 180 degrees.

Group: puts different text and images on a singular layer, and everything is moved at once so that it doesn't affect the layout.

Linetype: an option you can do with your piece, whether you want to cut a line, draw a bar, or score a sequence.

Mirrored image: reverses it, which is very important with transfer vinyl, so everything reads correctly.

Print then Cut: it's an option that lets you print the design, and from there, the machine cuts it.

Redo: does an action again and reverses it.

Reverse Weeding: removes the vinyl that's left behind, and it's used mostly for stencil vinyl

Score lines: helps you make creases in the papers so you can fold them.

SVG: this is a scalable vector graphic that lets you cut a file that's scaled to be larger or smaller so that the resolution is kept and made up of lines that consist of infinite white dots.

Texts and fonts: let you use put specialized fonts and words within Design Space.

Weeding: lets you remove the excess vinyl from designs. Press this when you're cutting vinyl.

Welding: a tool you use when you want to combine two-line shapes into one shape, and it's used to make seamless cursive words.

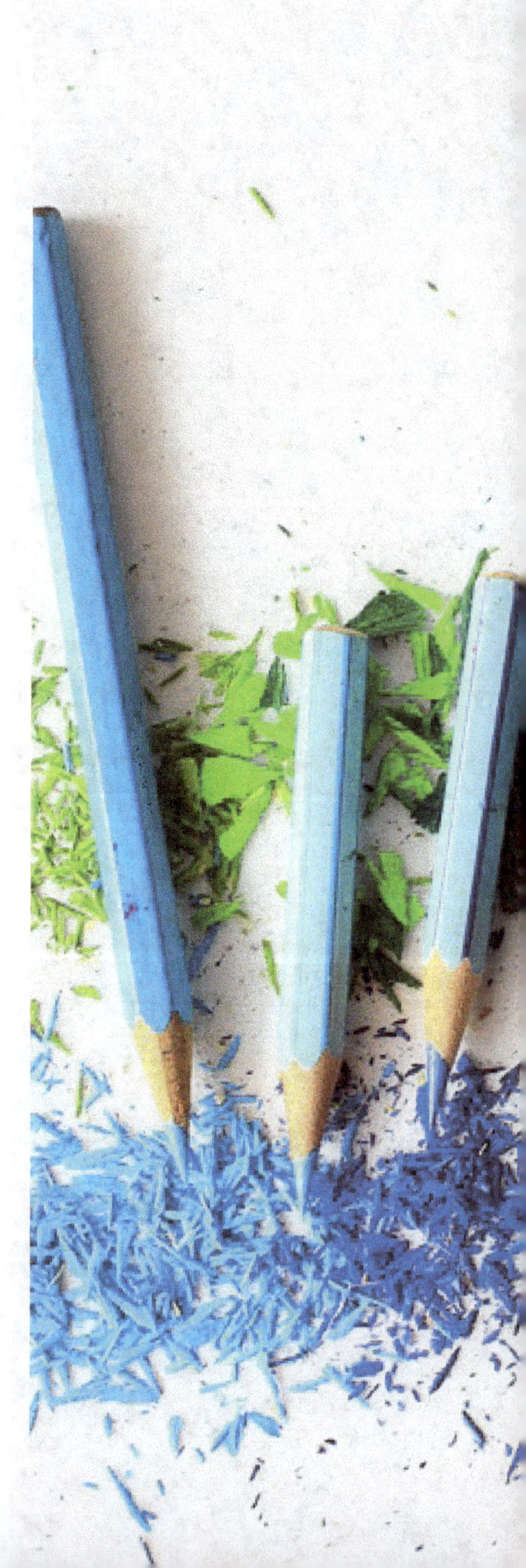

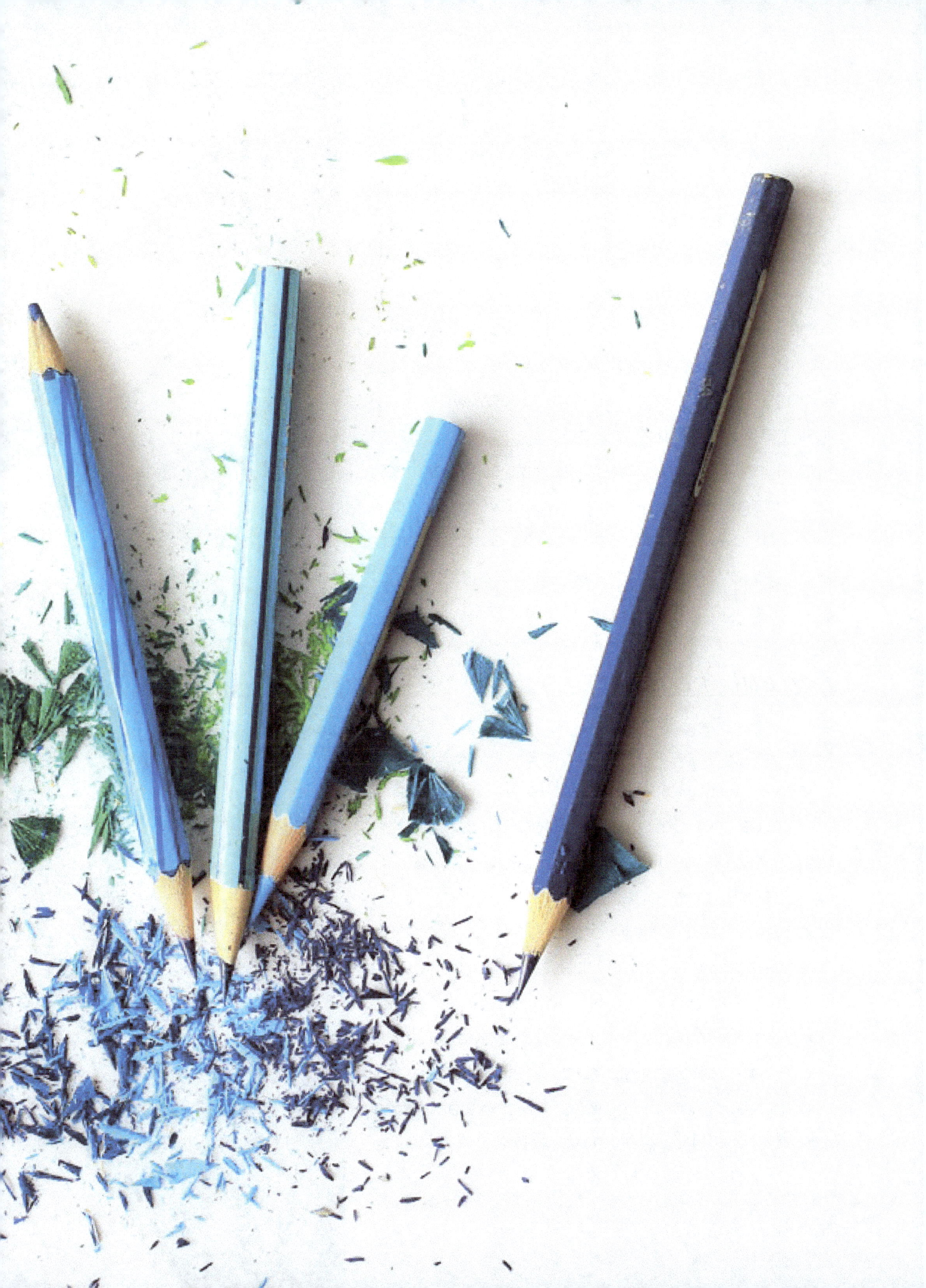

These are most of the functions you can do in Design Space. To use these, simply choose an image or font that you want to use and put it in Design Space. From there, you can do whatever you need to do with it - within reason, of course - and then place the image onto the material that you're using. You suggest not getting in too deep with vinyl just yet and getting used to using these tools for learning. You also have pens, which can be implemented to help you write images with a device that looks sharp and crisp. We'll go over the purpose of pens and what you can do with them in the next section.

Cricut Pens

Pens for your Cricut machine are essentially another way to get creative to use them for cards, handmade tags for gifts, or even fancy invites and labels.

Now, each pen offers a little different finish and point size. They aren't toxic, and they are permanent once they're dried. You've got the extra-fine points for small lettering, up to a medium tip for making thicker lines. There are also glitter and metallic pens, so you have a lot of options to choose from! But do you have to use them? Well, the

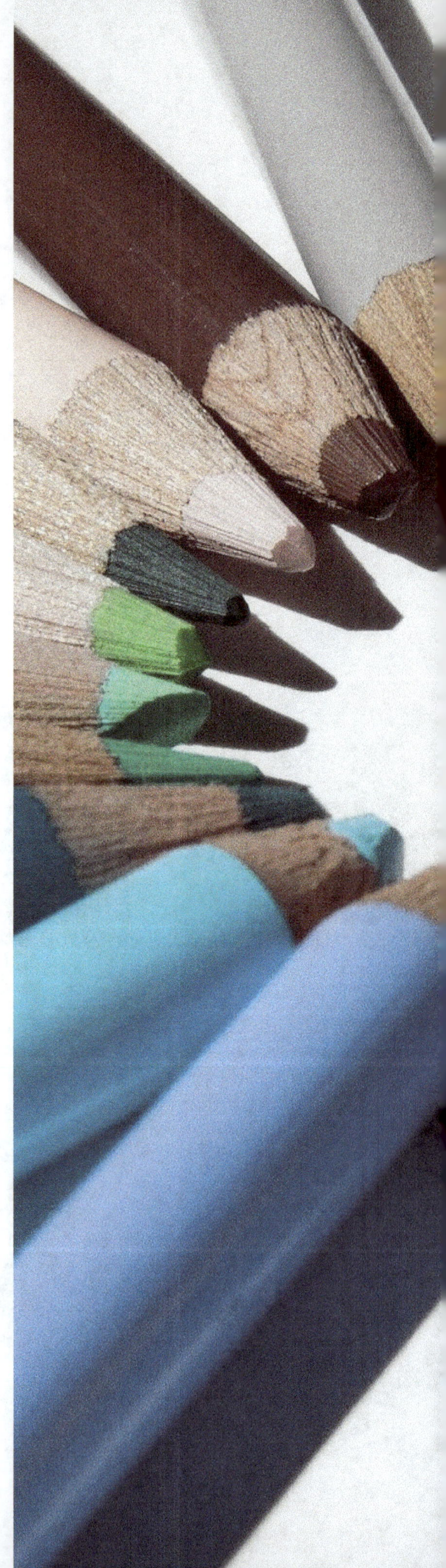

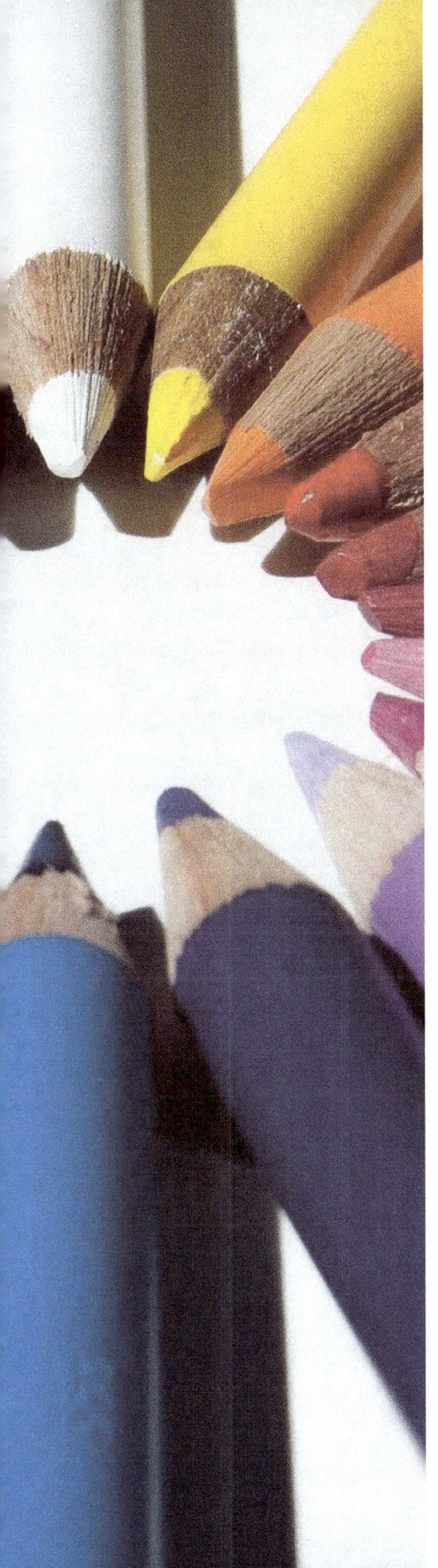

answer is no. You can use different pens but test them on paper first and get adapters to use with them. Cricut pens are your best option.

To use these, choose the wording or design or whatever you want to do. You want to go to the Layers panel on the right-hand side and select the scissors icon - change that to the write icon. From there, you'll want to choose the pen color that you would like to use.

You can then have the design printed out on the material you're using.

Some people like to use different fonts, whether it be system fonts or Cricut fonts, or the Cricut Access fonts. However, the one thing with Design Space is that it will write what will usually be cut, so you'll get an outline of that font rather than just a solid stroke of writing.

This can add to the design. However - you essentially change the machine from cut to write, and there you go.

You can also use the Cricut writing fonts, which you can choose by going to a blank canvas, and then selecting the text tool on the left-hand side, along with the wording you'd like for this to have.

Once you're in the font edit toolbar, you

are given a font selection. You choose the writing font filter, so you have fonts that you can write with. From there, choose the font, switch from the scissors to the pen icon, and then select the pen color. That's all there is to it!

You can also use this with Cricut Access - if you're planning on using this a lot, it might be worth it.

To insert the pens into the Cricut machine, you want to choose to make it, and from there, you'll then go to the prepare mat screen. It will say draw instead of writing in the thumbnail this time around, so you press continue in the bottom right-hand corner, then put the pen into clamp A - you just unlock it and then put it in. Wait until it clicks, and that's it!

Cricut pens are super easy, and it's a great idea to consider trying these out.

As you can see, there are many different Cricut features and a lot of functions that may seem complicated, but as you can see, you are not that hard. There are tons of options for your Cricut projects and a lot that you can get out of this machine.

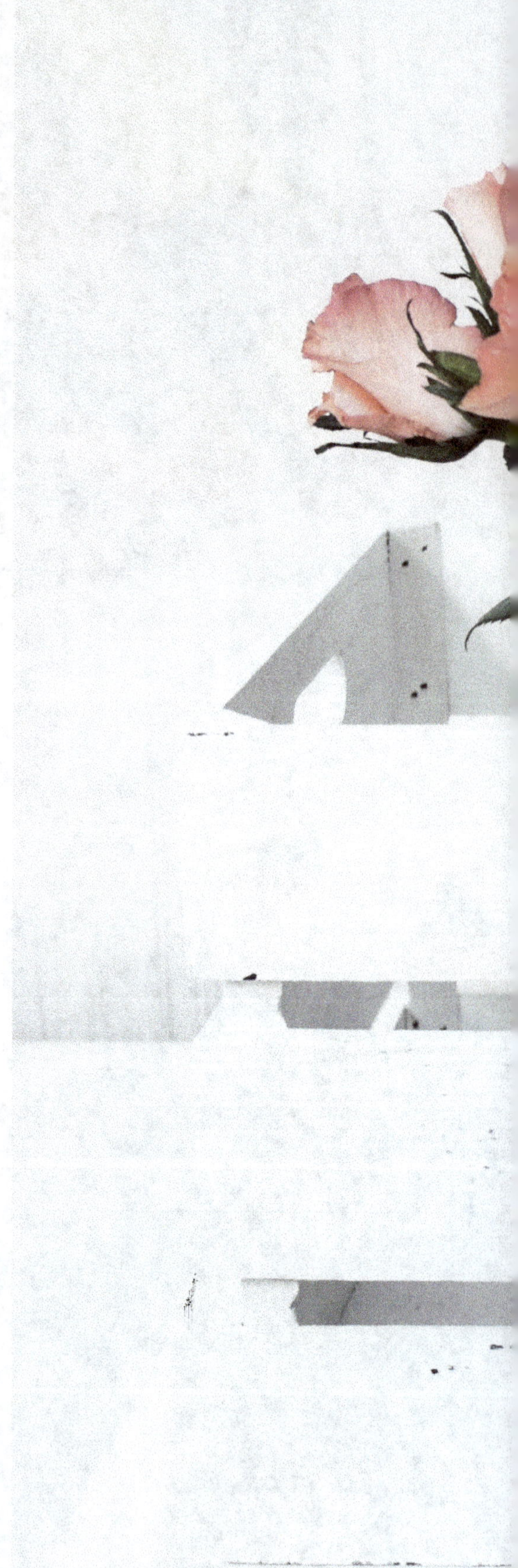

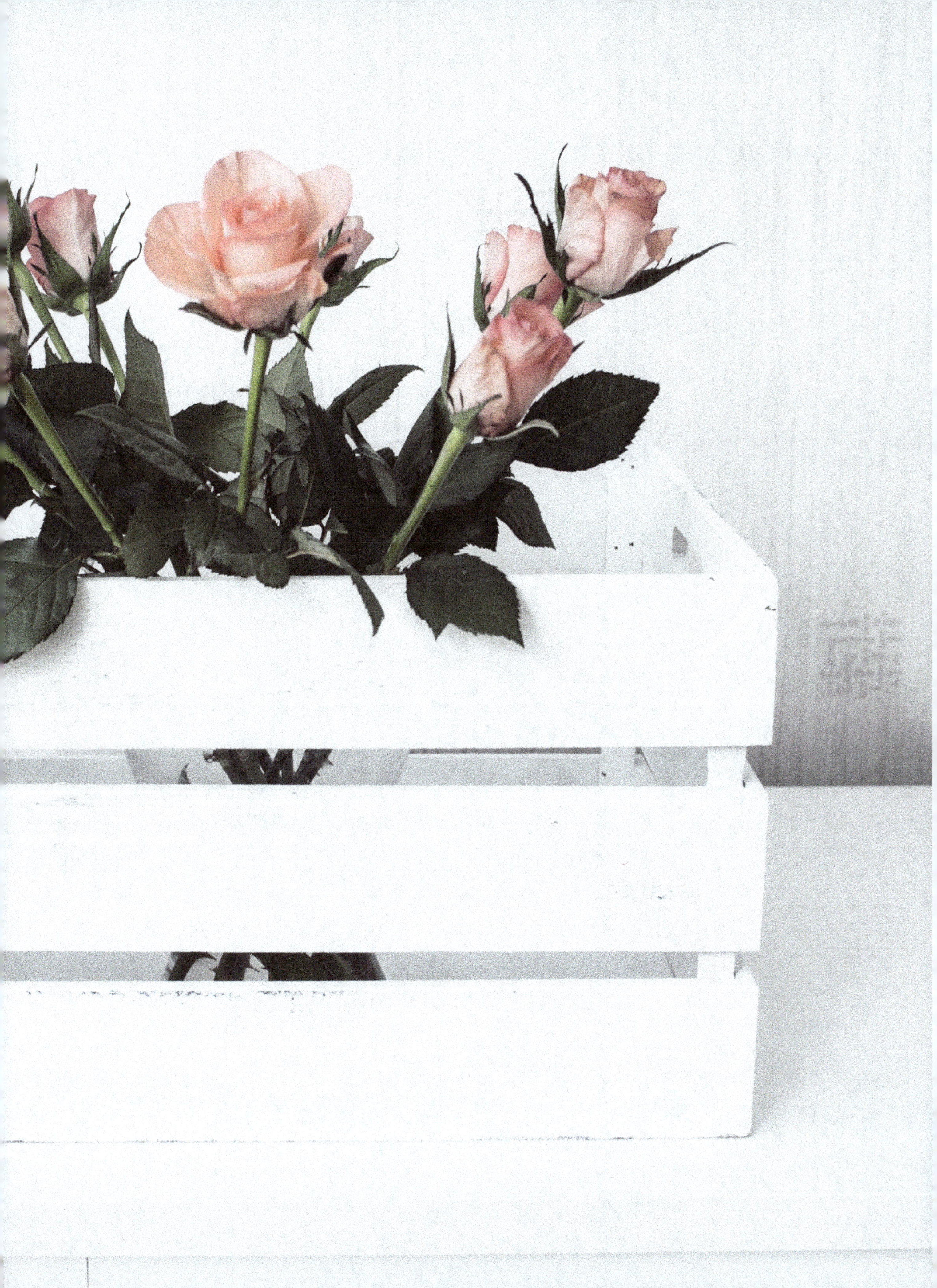

Conclusion

We have come to the end of our learning path in the world of Cricut, or rather, in the world of accessories that will simplify a lot of work and effort to create your crafts. I thank you once again for reading and purchasing my book.

Never stop doing research. Never stop trying new things. Never, ever stop being creative. The Cricut does not make you any less creative; it makes it easier to focus your valuable time and efforts on more important things or personalize the projects after making the cuts. It takes the tedious work out of your hands and makes everything fun, easy, and fast.

Cricut Machines make all projects and tasks related to cutting, tracking, and precision manufacturing simple. They give you the liberty to create any project, be it papercraft to vinyl decals.

All you have to do is connect your tablet, smartphone, or computer to a Cricut computer to get your project up and to run. There are various Cricut models to choose from if you're considering buying a Cricut for your home or business.

Everything on earth needs maintenance, including Cricut machines. These machines are continually cutting out materials of different textures, shapes, and quantities, etc. Thus, they need routine maintenance to boost their productivity levels and increase their life span.

The routine maintenance of these machines does not require a lot, and as a matter of fact, the hardware needs cleaning after cutting out materials. Thus, non-alcoholic baby wipes are highly recommended for cleaning material residue on the machines. The cutting mat is another item that needs maintenance from time to time because excessive usage without proper care reduces its stickiness.

When you purchase your Cricut machine, you will be excited to get started. Search the online Cricut library for ideas on creating cool projects that will make your environment more enjoyable and a project that you can use to give others joy in their life, such as cards and wooden signs.

The great thing about the Cricut is that you can use it with so many different materials that you will never run out of ideas for crafting and creating beautiful gifts.

Never stop doing research. Never stop trying new things. Never, ever stop being creative. The

Good luck with all your cutting projects.

Thank

you !!